The Greatest Book of Movie Lists in the World...Allegedly

Casey Heaton and Luke Worrell

Acknowledgements

We couldn't have written this book without help from some special people. Thank you to Lisa Steidinger for acting as editor, project manager and 15 other things on the project. Shout out to Dr. Christy Heaton for your edits and suggestions...the good ones and the bad ones. Big time thanks to our families, especially our wives. This book caused us to have a few late nights. Props to the 80's Co Host with the most...Lawrence Tucker.

Shout outs to...Taylor for taking in movies with me (even the ones you didn't want to see), Mr. Pete, The Validators, Sonny, Alec, our moms, Dusty, Vaughny, Kurt Russell and anyone who enjoys movies.

DEDICATION

For my Dad

**Who introduced me to movies and took me to Prestige
Video weekly, for various movie rentals.**

- Casey

Foreword

It was a dark and stormy night and Jessica Fletcher was sitting at her typewriter. Oh wrong book. Hi I'm Lawrence Tucker, if you don't know me I am one of the co hosts of The Awesome 80's Podcast, former pro wrestler and President of the Bloomington IL Murder She Wrote Fan Club. I have to say being asked to write this foreword was very humbling and yet very stressful. After reading through this book I realized it would be easier than I had originally thought. Casey and Luke are great story tellers. As a lover of both film and pro wrestling I look for a great story arc and these two magnificent gentlemen found a way to tell stories through lists... something BuzzFeed has been trying and failing at for 8 years.

To know why this book is special you have to know the authors. I first met this dynamic duo in a seafood restaurant in the middle of the French Quarter in New Orleans. My first thought after interacting with these two was, "Man these dudes are wasted." My second thought was "Do you think they will finish the crab? Is it rude if I ask for some?" After knowing them for a few months my thoughts changed to "Wow these are two of the funniest most genuine good brothers I have ever met."

Please sit back or down and enjoy this book as they both put great effort into composing the book while also telling a story about themselves throughout. Whether you read it in one sitting or in 15-20 minute chunks (wink) you will enjoy what these two gentlemen have to say. So chill out, crack open a Steveweiser and learn about everything from Cate Blanchett to Freddy Got Fingered and everything in between.

Greetings! First, let us say thank you from the bottom of our hearts for picking up this book. We truly hope you enjoy this book but if you don't...we don't want to hear about it. All joking aside, we created this writing project to entertain and inform. We hope that you walk away amused and also that you find new movies to watch or you recall movies that you have forgotten. We have been fans of film since children and we're guessing you are too. We hope you enjoy this journey you are about to embark upon.

Our Story: We've been best friends since high school, best men in each other's weddings, we played various sports together, we vacationed together, went to college together, we loved professional wrestling, and most importantly we watched many a movie together. We regularly debate film and actors (Affleck) and every year we send our top 25 movie rankings to each other. From those movie rankings an idea was born...why don't we rank them by genre?...or even actors?

So here we are...we've compiled a book of Top 5 lists in various genres. Some are traditional (Top 5 Christmas Movies) some are not (Top 5 Movies to Watch While Folding Laundry). We'll share some of our favorite actors/actresses, directors, various other themes and we'll walk you through our favorite movies from 1980-2017. We provided our honest opinions on each film named, but remember these are just the opinions of a couple of 30 something year old Nerd-Dads.

Happy Reading,

Casey and Luke

"Whether you like it or not, learn to love it, because it's the best thing going...WHOO!"
-Ric Flair

Table of Contents

1. Actors & Directors

In this section, you will find our top 5 favorite films of several actors, actresses and directors. Some of them may be our favorites...some of them are definitely not our favorites. We really tried to avoid using all of our favorite people and to mix it up a bit. We also really needed to find people that had directed or starred in a lot of movies. In addition, you will find a special list where we cast the roles of our very own Biopic. Enjoy!

(C) = Casey
(L) = Luke

Actors that would Star in My Biopic (C)

1. Michael Fassbender – I think this dude is a fantastic actor and he would be my top choice. I think I'd play the "we both have Irish ancestry" card. Sometimes I picture myself as Magneto.
2. Chris Pratt – Pratt is probably a better choice for me though, he can play the funny goofball pretty easily and still make it charming. And yes I'm claiming to be a charming funny goofball. I'm sure there's a lot of eye rolling happening right now.
3. Ryan Gosling – I just like to think I'm this handsome. But in all seriousness he is a pretty good actor. Recently enjoyed him in Blade Runner 2049 (2017).
4. James Roday – James is known for his role on TV's "Psych" but I think he'd be a good fit for me. His love of the 80's and general Pop Culture knowledge is an easy match. I remember discovering him in Rolling Kansas (2003) as it was showing on Comedy Central back in the day.
5. Jonah Hill – This one is more of a shot at my wife (assuming she reads this). So I posed this very question to her one day while road tripping and she had the gall to say Jonah Hill. It wasn't even skinny Jonah Hill. Her reasoning was because he is super funny and can also do more serious parts. Nice try. I will never let her forget this one.

Actors that would Star in My Biopic (L)

1. Matt Damon. I like Matt Damon. Seems like a good dude. This is where good reasons for him playing me end. He is too good looking and too talented but it is Hollywood so let's try to make Luke Worrell look good.

2. Will Ferrell. He is taller and a shameless clown. Tall and Shameless Clown are the top two adjectives used to describe me so this makes sense.

3. Jason Bateman. I name him for many of the reasons I named for Matt Damon. Just seems like a good dude. This is a movie book but without Arrested Development, I probably wouldn't name him here. Really became a huge fan of Jason's there.

4. John Krasinski. I like to think that ole John and I would have a lot in common. Seems nice, personable and quirky.

5. Paul Rudd. Obviously none of these guys look like me but I am going with guys I have respect for. Please keep in mind I couldn't quite tell you why I respect them so yep....this list is weird.

Drew Barrymore (C)

1. E.T. (1982) – Who can forget cute little Drew in E.T.? It's beside the point that I think this movie is overrated, but you simply cannot ignore the adorable performance by Drew at the age of seven!

2. The Wedding Singer (1998) – I'll admit it right now I don't love a lot of Drew movies...but there is something special about her and Sandler in this one. She just seemed like an all around great girl. So glad she didn't become Julia Gulia.

3. Fever Pitch (2005) – Throwing this on the list because my bro-in-law is a Sox fan. Solid flick. Thought Drew and Fallon had some good chemistry and it's a baseball movie. Drew basically ended the curse.

4. Scream (1996) – When I first saw this I was shocked that Drew didn't survive the opening scene. What a genius move killing off the most notable star of the film. Also her name was Casey in the film so she gets bonus points.

5. Music and Lyrics (2007) – Real fun movie to round out my top five. Really felt like Drew and Hugh Grant had a blast making the picture.

Drew Barrymore (L)

1. E.T. (1982) -You know what I realized? I don't have much Drew Barrymore experience. For some strange reason, I have not seen many of her movies, even her famous ones. My apologies Drew, it isn't personal or intentional. ET is kind of #1 by default here. Not only do I remember watching this with my big sister growing up, but I dug the ride at Universal Studios as well.

2. The Wedding Singer (1998) - A very good comedy before Sandler's star started to fade in my opinion. Drew had a good little stretch here. Disclaimer: I never saw 50 First Dates which many say is the superior Sandler/Barrymore film.

3. Never Been Kissed (1999) - A teeny bopper chick flick but guess when I watched it? That's right, when I was a teen. You know what you do when you're 18 and a girl you kind of have a crush on suggests you rent this and watch it? You watch the friggin' film. It wasn't bad.

4. Whip It (2009) - I think people slept on this one. Roller Derby theme and has a sprinkling of Kristen Wiig. Smashley Simpson is a pretty good character name as well.

5. Wayne's World 2 (1993) - I probably shouldn't even count this as it was a brief cameo but her delivery was great and I remember this part of the movie so distinctly. Much like Wayne Cambell, I also know a lot about Sweden without actually having been there.

Cate Blanchett (C)

1. The Curious Case of Benjamin Button (2008) - This is a great story. Brad Pitt was really good in this but Cate was even better. They took a great concept and delivered with a very strong performance. But it's so depressing when you realize Brad and Cate's relationship days are numbered. Also to be noted my wife called this movie "Emotionally Mute" after I nearly cried.

2. Lord of the Rings (2001) Her role as Galadriel, even though small, was very impactful. Cate had an amazing presence in the trilogy and was super impressive and intimidating all at the same time.

3. The Missing (2003) – What a character transformation. I didn't even realize this was Cate when I first watched this movie. Powerful performance in a strange flick.

4. Robin Hood (2010) – A slower paced Robin Hood film but great performances from Cate and Crowe. Cate was a great Marion and has an unintentionally funny scene of leading kids into battle on ponies...for real life.

5. Indiana Jones and the Kingdom of the Crystal Skull (2008) – Just hear me out. Yes this movie is a turd. One thing I enjoyed while watching was Cate as Irina Spalko. Thought she did a bang up job on a bad script with a bad cast.

Cate Blanchett (L)

1. Elizabeth (1998) - This is the first film I remember of Cate's. I had not heard of her up to this point. I think it is without a doubt, her best work and what I think of first and foremost. It actually triggered in me an interest in English history which up to that point, I cared for about as much as mustard, baked beans, and grits.

2. The Missing (2003) - This placement is based on sentimental memory. I saw this with one of my top 50 friends, Casey Heaton, in South Padre Island, Texas. Perhaps it's the overall trip I remember the most fondly but it sticks out still in 2018.

3. The Life Aquatic with Steve Zissou (2004) - I have no idea why but I find this moving hysterical. Having said that, I honestly am completely unimpressed with all other Wes Anderson films. Fun fact: I bought this on DVD and leant it to the PA announcer of the South Bend Silverhawks and then forgot to get it back before my internship ended. I play "Taps" for that copy once a year every summer…..

4. Babel (2006) - A darling of the critics, it is a movie that makes you think and feel. Sometimes those suck, this particular film was enjoyable and made a vivid impression on me. Some scenes are troubling. I also ponder how many people miss the biblical reference in the title.

5. Monuments Men (2014) - I thought this movie would be more captivating honestly, but it still was a really enjoyable piece with an A+ cast. I can always get behind history and Paris, France. Viva la France.

Sandra Bullock (C)

1. Demolition Man (1993) – Rumor has it Lori Petty was originally cast...thank goodness it didn't work out. Sandra was fabulous in this role and used it as her spring board into Hollywood stardom. Seeing young innocent Sandra in this film just brings a smile to my face.
2. Speed (1994) – Following her success from Demo Man, she hopped on board (a bus) with Keanu. Another great role for Sandra as she climbed the ladder.
3. While You Were Sleeping (1995) – My sister loved this movie, so I think I just mindlessly watched it a few too many times. Sandra was on fire. She just kept putting out hits.
4. The Lake House (2006) – The reunion of Sandra and Keanu for a sort of sci-fi love story...just not much sci-fi...I guess more of just a magic mail box. Really liked the storyline and performance.
5. A Time to Kill (1996) – Sandra was so hot in the 90's she could do no wrong...except for the Net (1995). That was very wrong. Great move on her part though getting attached to the Grisham novel pictures. She turned in the best performance amongst some good acting.

Sandra Bullock (L)

1. A Time to Kill (1996) - One of my top 25 favorite films. Powerful stuff. A young Sandra wasn't the headliner but she was really coming into her own here. The material doesn't lend itself to humor but this film gives me all the feels.

2. Speed (1994) - She did films prior to this but this was when Sandra became a household name in my opinion. Forget the abomination that was Speed 2 (1997) and just enjoy this film with a passable Keanu and a devilish Dennis Hopper. Even my boy Jeff Daniels showed up. I have never viewed the Arizona Wildcats the same. You'll never catch me on a bus in Tempe, Arizona.

3. The Blind Side (2009) - A touching football movie. So Michael Oher says a lot of it was hogwash...it still packed a punch and is still the only proof that Nick Saban has a personality. Getting off subject....I can't take Tim McGraw seriously as an actor. He isn't bad, I just can't get past it and I'm constantly waiting for a musical ensemble.

4. Gravity (2013) - This garnered some buzz a few years back and I really enjoyed it. A great cast + space = solid movie...it is scientifically factual.

5. Forces of Nature (1999) - OK, I have some explaining to do. This is not on here because Casey's favorite Ben Affleck is the lead. I was 17 many moons ago and on a cruise. Back then, you had a movie channel on cruises that essentially showed the same 3 movies on a loop. I was young and trying to figure out life and women at the same time. Darn it if I didn't watch this chick flick 6 times over that cruise.....

Nicolas Cage (C)

1. National Treasure (2004) – First off let me say I love that Cage is in the book. Secondly...I don't really like Nic Cage. Third I think he has done many...many interesting films. Let me start with a movie that I think is actually fantastic. National Treasure is a fun action/adventure/comedy with a nice blend of "History". A great movie that inspired treasure hunters all around the world.

2. The Rock (1996) – Another really awesome movie and if I'm being honest...Connery steals the show. Cage was also really good though. Stanley Goodspeed is an amazing character name. I really wish he would have shared the secret of the Kennedy assassination at the end.

3. Con Air (1997) – Alright now we get into "Awesomely Bad" territory now. What a great idea...a hijacked plane full of convicts and only one man can save them...Nicolas Cage. Guilty pleasure of mine. "Put the bunny back in the box."

4. Face/Off (1997) – This movie is legit insane. Over acting at its finest between Cage and Travolta. Another great concept with absolutely insane character choices. Must see.

5. Raising Arizona (1987) – A classic Cage 80's flick. I didn't see this until recently and I really enjoyed it. Thought Cage was really strong in this flick and it makes me sad to see him putting out crap these days.

Nicolas Cage (L)

1. National Treasure (2004) - I really slept on this movie and then was blown away by how much I enjoyed it. Even if the actual story is mostly historical fabrication, the cast was great and it was good ole fashioned entertainment. It really gets the mind going. I fought the urge to not become a conspiracy theorist after seeing it.

2. The Rock (1996) - This movie was awesome in junior high. I would say it ages well too. He might have had a ton of help from Sir Sean Connery and Sir Ed Harris (disclaimer: Ed is not actually knighted) but this movie was so good at the time when I was in the dead center of puberty and adolescence.

3. It Could Happen to You (1994) - A departure from the typical Nic Cage film here. Every now and then you need a feel good story without death and bloodshed. Not often, but occasionally. I really liked this one as a change of pace Nic film back when you know...he didn't make awful movies.

4. Face/Off (1997) - Cage and John Travolta were huge stars when this movie was made. Let that sink in and feel old for a while. A really good premise and solid action. "I must become him."

5. Con-Air (1997) - This doesn't age well at all. His accent is terrible and the story sucks but I was 15 when this came out so I get a pass. What the heck happened to Nicolas Cage? He actually had a really good run of movies and then just one day woke up and said, "I am going to try and make 18 awful films this year."

Tom Cruise (C)

1. Top Gun (1986) – I feel like if you asked 100 people to name their favorite Tom Cruise movie…100 people would say Top Gun. And I am no different! Cruise rules in this movie as a young cocky pilot trying to bed the instructor. It's safe to say this movie takes my breath away. Count it.

2. Mission Impossible (1996) – I feel the movie was probably pitched like this…"It's a Tom Cruise action thriller with a catchy theme song". And then someone with a lot of money was like "I love it, why don't we just remake the old Mission Impossible show?" I'm pretty sure that's how it went down. Needless to say Tom is a great Ethan Hunt.

3. Jerry Maguire (1996) "Show me the money." 96 was a good year for Tom. All I'm saying is if I was a professional athlete I definitely would have stuck with Jerry. A lot of iconic lines from this movie and the little kid with the big head almost stole the spotlight from Tom…almost.

4. Edge of Tomorrow (2014) – Most you are probably questioning a movie from this decade breaking into my top 5…but I would then challenge you to see the movie. It's fantastic. Great story and even better performance from Tom. I feel like he really solidified that he can still make a good flick. Didn't hurt having Emily Blunt around as well.

5. Cocktail (1988) – Tom Cruise + Elisabeth Shue + Jamaica = me, being in a very, very good mood. Pretty dark ending but Tom carries the picture into my top 5.

Tom Cruise (L)

1. Top Gun (1986) - I would wager many people would have the same answer here. It truly is Tom's iconic role, at least for people my age. Goose dying (spoiler!) was one of the first traumatic movie experiences I remember as a child. Also, how cool was Val Kilmer? Ice Man was almost too cool. Hard to hate that guy.

2. Jerry Maguire (1996) - A great love and personal journey story centered around sports? Sign me up! Cuba Gooding Jr. was sensational and it was well before he started making crap like Snow Dogs (2002). So many memorable lines and scenes not to mention a ballad by Bruce Springsteen on the sound track!

3. Far and Away (1992) - A double VHS tape rental from back in the day. Long but worth it and an excellent story. History pieces have proven to sway me and this is no exception. I also must admit that I never saw Days of Thunder so this was my first experience with Nicole Kidman as well.

4. Rain Man (1988) - This movie came out in 1988. I first saw this movie around 20 years later. Better late than never right! A young Tom with the world as his oyster. I dug the story and performance. It also finally made that one Hangover (2009) scene funnier to me.

5. Magnolia (1999) - Have you ever had a movie that you really liked but can't give one good reason as to why? This is a perfect example of that. This movie was weird and 85% depressing. Yet somehow at the end of the movie (right after I asked myself what I just saw) I realized I really liked it. I couldn't argue as to why but here it is ahead of the likes of Collateral (2004), The Last Samurai (2003), Jack Reacher (2012) and others.

Harrison Ford (C)

1. Indiana Jones and the Last Crusade (1989) - This might be unpopular with the masses, but this is my favorite Harrison performance AND Indiana Jones movie. I enjoy this one over Raiders, but most likely because I was 7 when I first saw this. When I go back and watch these films I always feel like Harrison is having the most fun on this movie. I'm sure I'll find out he hated working on this movie now. Fun Fact: The Indiana Jones Theme is my dad's ringtone to this day.

2. Star Wars (1977) – Han Solo is one of the coolest characters in cinema history…it is undisputable. Solo shot first.

3. Clear and Present Danger (1994) – The Jack Ryan movies were all very well done but I think this is better than Patriot Games (1992). And to be clear Harrison Ford is the only real Jack Ryan. Actually Chris Pine was ok.

4. Six Days and Seven Nights (1998) – This is a fun island romp with Harrison and Anne Heche…yup. Ford is a totally believable boozed up island pilot. My mom once famously referred to this movie as Eight Days and Five Nights.

5. Air Force One (1997) – Great flick and the best fictitious movie president out there. This is about Harrison but Gary Oldman was pretty good as well. No one throws terrorists off of planes quite like old Harrison.

Harrison Ford (L)

1. The Fugitive (1993) - Occasionally I fight the urge to scream about "Provasic" while in Walgreens. Then I realize a whole generation after me might not get the joke. This movie was awesome and him playing off of Tommy Lee Jones even though they rarely shared the screen was amazing. I also have never trusted someone with one arm since.

2. Empire Strikes Back (1980) - Ole Harry's filmography is arguably deeper than anyone else's. He was simply on fire from the late 70's to the mid 90's. Han Solo is my favorite character of his and this is my favorite Star Wars film. It makes sense.

3. Indiana Jones and the Last Crusade (1989) - I don't know if it is Sean Connery but I always seemed to like this one the best. I mean the Holy Grail....I am a believer and a history guy so I really loved them going back to biblical artifacts.

4. Clear and Present Danger (1994) - I watched this in the theater with my dad. He had to fill in a bit of the lines regarding political mind games but I do distinctly remember this movie experience. Willem DaFoe was glorious as well. That pairing hit my fancy.

5. Return of the Jedi (1983) - I am a Star Wars guy raising a Star Wars guy in my oldest son Kale. While he digs the new generation of films. I am still partial to the ones of my childhood.

Ryan Gosling (C)

1. The Nice Guys (2016) – Really liked him in this 70's version of Lethal Weapon. Wasn't your typical Gosling, he's a great imperfect protagonist. He and Crowe worked really well together, great comeback movie for Shane Black.
2. Crazy Stupid Love (2011) – Pretty solid RomCom with a stand out performance from Gosling. He's great in the mentor role for picking up chicks. Also, he and Emma Stone nail that Dirty Dancing (1987) routine.
3. La La Land (2016) - Took my wife to see this in theaters. She had been wanting to see it so badly. Coming away I think I liked it better than she did. Gosling and Stone clearly have great onscreen chemistry. Cool story with some good tunes. They were robbed of the Oscar…literally. Gosling is cast so perfectly, he seems like a local artist who has dreams of doing his own thing. I was enthralled.
4. The Notebook (2004) - I hate to admit this BUT…what a great story. Gosling and McAdams really deliver. Saw this one in the weirdest movie theater of all time…I think it was a converted barn theater.
5. Blade Runner 2049 (2017) - Saw this in theaters. Thought it was a good sequel to the original. Gosling was pretty good in a very different role for him. Spoiler alert…he is a Replicant in the movie…which some would argue that isn't a tough role…but I thought he nailed it.

Ryan Gosling (L)

1. The Notebook (2004) - This movie holds a special place in my heart and it isn't because of Rachel McAdams this time. I took my wife to see this on her 20th birthday while I was an intern in South Bend, Indiana. We went out to a fancy dinner and then saw this romantic film. Pure Emotion. Darn you Nicholas Sparks.

2. Crazy Stupid Love (2011) - A great cast and I found this movie hysterical. I never knew that I would laugh so hard at Ryan Gosling punching Kevin Bacon. A great rental.

3. Half Nelson (2006) - A very raw and gritty indie movie. I would imagine many haven't seen this one but it was very real. Depressing......but real.

4. Ides of March (2011) - A political thriller with an outrageously good cast. The ups and downs of this movie have you on a roller coaster. I think this one slipped past people as well. This is one people need to see, especially in an election year. You'll want to leave the U.S., but still...

5. Fracture (2007) - An intellectual thriller. These are right up my alley. Anthony Hopkins was great as well and he didn't even have to eat anybody. Looking back at Ryan Gosling's work, there are still plenty I need to catch up on but I think he is high quality. Not just a dreamy face.

Tom Hanks (C)

1. Big (1988) - Pre 90's Tom Hanks is one of the greatest things since sliced bread. I like to refer to 80's Tom as the funny years. This is a great story where a 13 year old wishes to grow up and figures out the harsh realities of being an adult. I've actually been looking for a Zoltar machine to become a kid again.

2. Catch Me if You Can (2002) - Incredible film based on a true story about a professional con man. Tom Hanks and Leonardo DiCaprio are fantastic in this movie. They both should have beat Adrian Brody in the Pianist (2002) for the Oscar. Tom Hanks' Carl Hanratty steals the show.

3. A League of Their Own (1992) – Tom has a great performance as the manager of the Rockford Peaches. A great story of women's baseball during World War II and Tom leads the way.

4. Toy Story (1995) – This seems like somewhat of a cheat...since it's only Tom's voice. But Woody has become one of Tom's most iconic roles especially if you're a millennial. I may have been a little too old for this when it came out but that didn't stop me from loving it one bit. I've always loved the idea of toys coming to life. It's such a great concept and Pixar really nailed it. Side note: Have y'all read Indian in the Cupboard?

5. Dragnet (1988) – Used to watch the show on Nick at Night back in the day...and even though the show was boring...this movie rules. This may even be Tom's funniest flick. This is one of those fun movies you can watch at any moment and it's a blast. I feel this was the source material for Zootopia (2016).

Tom Hanks (L)

1. Saving Private Ryan (1998) - Full disclosure...you'll see this on a lot of lists. I would have loved the movie without Tom Hanks but no way it casts as heavy as a punch if someone else was in that role.

2. Apollo 13 (1995) - Is there a better movie to reference while playing six degrees of Kevin Bacon? I digress.....Factual dramas are my jam, kind of like mint chocolate chip ice cream. Apollo 13 is one of those movies where if you are flipping channels and it is on, soooo hard not to stop right there and enjoy it.

3. Forrest Gump (1994) - Tom's most iconic role? A movie unlike any other. This will put you in a glass case of emotion. Sidebar....I have been to Savannah, GA and sat at that bus stop. Cool little moment.

4. You've Got Mail (1998) - This is my wife's favorite movie. It's at the point where I actually enjoy watching her watch the movie more than watching it myself. It has to be on my list. I don't want to have to explain myself if she reads this list and wonders WTH...

5. A League of their Own (1992) - I kid you not, I watched this VHS 292 times at my Grandparents' house as a child. The whole cast was sensational. I kind of want a Rockford Peaches hat to be honest with you. RIP Jimmy Dugan.

John Hughes (C)

1. Weird Science (1985) – This may have been the toughest list to compile. To me John Hughes' films are all A+'s. So, this is how it all shakes out if I really must rank them 1-5. I love Wyatt and Gary but if I'm really being honest this is my #1 because of Kelly LeBrock and her Shermer High PE Attire.
2. Breakfast Club (1985) - I remember watching this movie for the first time with my older cousins and thinking I was so damn cool. Is this what high school was like in the 80's? In my mind…yes. John Hughes nailed it. What iconic characters. Kind of messed up they made the nerd finish the assignment. "Don't mess with the bull young man, you'll get the horns."
3. Sixteen Candles (1985) – I was late to the party on Sixteen Candles. Not sure how this slipped by, I've always been a big John Hughes fan. I'd always thought this was a "chick flick" for some reason. Oddly enough it was my wife who informed of the greatness. Watched it a few years ago and loved it. Some pretty dark stuff going on in the periphery though. Also, I'm assuming Jake Ryan had bad intentions.
4. Ferris Bueller's Day Off (1986) – As a kid I often fantasized about having an epic Ferris Bueller type day of playing hooky. Long story short…I never came close. I am honestly too lazy to even attempt what Ferris did. I feel like most people are familiar with the awesomeness of this film so I would just like to highlight my favorite part…Sloane Peterson.
5. Uncle Buck (1989) – It is crazy to me that Hughes only directed 8 movies because he wrote for so many other great flicks. Uncle Buck rounds out my list behind a great performance from John Candy. I recently went to a fund raiser at an elementary school and whilst using the tiny urinals I was reminded of the classic scene of Candy on one knee while peeing in the elementary school bathroom.

John Hughes (L)

1. Breakfast Club (1985) - The ultimate coming of age story that is timeless. Sure high school looks different throughout the eras but many of the issues involved in the story stay the same. What a cast! Who would have thought the stressed out wrestling star would end up being a great youth Hockey coach!

2. Ferris Bueller's Day Off (1986) - Epic. I can't see these actors even today all grown up without flashing back to this one. True Story, I have a farm listed right now for a Mueller family. I have to give myself a pep talk every time not to call them Bueller.

3. Planes, Trains and Automobiles (1987) - Timeless classic. I can't help but think of it every time I fly out of Lambert Airport. I haven't seen it in some time but always think of it fondly.

4. Uncle Buck (1989) - I remember seeing this one a little too young. Looking back now as an adult it just keeps getting better and funnier with time.

5. Sixteen Candles (1985) - Molly Ringwald. What a star of the 80's. I remember appreciating this as a kiddo and remember my sister watching it on repeat.

Samuel L. Jackson (C)

1. Jurassic Park (1993) – "Hold on to your butts". Even with a smaller role Sam Jackson is one of my favorite characters in this movie. I thought Sam and the game warden were out shined by Jeff Goldblum who garnered most of the attention. Poor Mr. Arnold.

2. Pulp Fiction (1994) – This may be the movie for which Sam is most known. Jules Winnfield is one of the coolest hitmen to ever grace the big screen. He and Travolta nailed it with these performances. He had a great presence and an even better look. Now for the million dollar question...does Jules say Brad or Brett? "Check out the big brain on B_____." Mysteries of the universe.

3. The Hateful Eight (2015) – Another Sam/Tarrantino collaboration. I love Sam as the bounty hunter going after confederates. Kurt Russell in a support role was pretty bad ass as well. This movie gave me a big The Thing (1982) vibe. A lot of similarities.

4. Die Hard with a Vengeance (1995) – What a great installment to the Die Hard franchise. Way better than the second and right on par with the first. This is around the time I started taking notice of Samuel L. Jackson. I really wish the Die Hard series had ended here. "No he said Hey...Zeus."

5. Snakes on a Plane (2006) – Let me start off with a fun fact. I saw this movie on a plane. I remember we were about to land in Sydney and the film ended like seconds before the plane turned off all electronics. I also vividly remember receiving a voicemail from Sam L Jackson telling me that Snakes on a Plane was going to be the best effin movie of the Summer. Luke heard it as well.

Samuel L. Jackson (L)

1. **A Time to Kill (1996)** - A movie that brings the emotion and drama and will leave you with a solitary tear streaming down your face. I loved the movie then and now. An easy choice for me.

2. **Pulp Fiction (1994)** - I am not as huge of a Pulp fan as most, but Sammy was great here. His credit list is immense but I bet you this is one most people identify him with. I also must say that if I didn't have that Cypress Hill CD with his speech before one of the tracks, this would probably be #3 or #4.

3. **Unbreakable (2000)** - I enjoyed "Mr. Glass" although this movie went mostly unheralded. He and Bruce played well off each other. I rented this and watched it late one night while at Lake of the Ozarks.

4. **Resurrecting the Champ (2007)** - I think this gets overlooked but I really enjoyed the premise. A tough one to watch in some respects because the plight of the homeless is hard to get over. Off topic, where the heck is Josh Hartnett? That guy disappeared faster than this morning's dew.

5. **The Negotiator (1998)** - A solid flick right in the middle of a solid run by both he and Kevin Spacey. I remember renting this at Family Video and watching it one night when I should have probably been doing homework.

Tommy Lee Jones (C)

1. Under Siege (1992) – Even though Tommy wasn't the lead in this, he was an excellent bad guy. When I first saw this as a kid I knew Tommy wasn't one to mess with. Bandana and aviators was a great look for TLJ.

2. The Fugitive (1993) – I feel like this role is what Tommy will always be remembered for. Pretty iconic role but I prefer him in Under Siege. "What I want from each and every one of you is a hard-target search of every gas station, residence, warehouse, farmhouse, henhouse, outhouse and doghouse in that area."

3. Men in Black (1997) – He played second fiddle to Will Smith but he brought plenty to the table. He played crusty old man very well.

4. Blown Away (1994) – Somehow talked my dad into taking me to see Blown Away in theaters. I'll never forget Tommy as a crazy Irish bomber. Really good performance.

5. U.S. Marshals (1998) – The Sam Gerard character was such a hit they made another movie. Pretty good flick. Downey Jr and Wesley Snipes with some nice roles as well. I really don't have much else to say on Tommy.

Tommy Lee Jones (L)

1. The Fugitive (1993) - The distance between this and #2 is immense. This is such a good movie in so many ways. I immediately think of Tommy Lee Jones when I hear this title uttered. Tommy Lee and Harrison are dual good guys pitted on opposite sides which was incredibly compelling.

2. Lincoln (2012) - A period piece that is right up my alley. No rhyme or reason to place this fun fact here but did you know Tommy Lee went to Harvard on a football scholarship and was roommates with Al Gore? Fascinating.

3. Blown Away (1994) - Incredibly underrated action flick from the 90's. Tommy is one of those guys who is as good of a bad guy as anything. The slow-motion view of him on the boat near the end...spectacular.

4. No Country for Old Men (2007) - While he isn't the first actor you think of here, heck he might not even be in the top three, it is still a movie that sticks with you. While the ending was pretty "meh", Mr. Jones played a big part in this movie being captivating.

5. Under Siege (1992) - Apparently, I love a "heel" Tommy Lee Jones. He just does gruff butt kicker so well...

Julia Roberts (C)

1. My Best Friend's Wedding (1997) – Ol' Julia is a National Treasure and more known for a different movie but this is my favorite of hers. The whole movie centers around Julia trying to break up a marriage. I swear it's a comedy. Great musical dinner scene.
2. Pretty Woman (1990) – Pretty Woman put Julia on the map and showed us the lighter side of prostitution. Good for you Julia.
3. The Pelican Brief (1993) – This is kind of a sentimental pick. I enjoy the story and Denzel teaming up with Julia and the dad from Home Alone (1990). But my fondest memories are of watching this movie with my dad and sister.
4. Ocean's Eleven (2001) – I just feel cool when I watch this movie. One of the best heist movies out there with an All-Star cast. Danny Ocean is so lucky to have Tess in his life.
5. Erin Brockovich (2000) – Saw this in theaters with my cousin Katie. And I will go on record saying Julia in 2000 was the hottest she had ever been. What's that have to do with her acting performance? Nothing...just wanted you all to know where I stand on the matter. Having said that she did an amazing job as Erin B bringing down that the power company.

Julia Roberts (L)

1. Pretty Woman (1990) - I would argue this is THE role Julia Roberts is known for. Princess Vivian was a great ending. A talented beauty, Miss Roberts was on fire in that early 90's period. Two negatives from the film. It was hard to see George Costanza be a huge jerk. Again, the real losers here are the actual prostitutes out there. There had to be that one idiot who thought they actually looked like Julia Roberts….

2. Pelican Brief (1993) - Denzel and Julia at the height of their powers was a dynamic combination. The thinking man thriller is a favorite genre of mine as well. I recently re-watched and it holds up!

3. Hook (1991) - This movie means a lot to me. My dad took me when I was a wee boy and it holds a special place in my heart. A tiny little Julia nailed Tinkerbell and I am forever grateful. RIP Rufio.

4. Erin Brockovich (2000) - Julia played this feisty role to a T. She nailed it and got an Oscar nod in the process. I have a feeling this might be higher if I re-watched it. I honestly saw this once and haven't gone back in time.

5. Conspiracy Theory (1997) - Another dynamic combo with Julia and Mel Gibson. It really helped that this was made before Mel went through four consecutive mid-life crisis's in succession as well. I miss Julia Roberts. She pops up here and there but her 1990-2000 was loaded with the goods excluding a marriage to Lyle Lovett.

Arnold Schwarzenegger (C)

1. Terminator 2: Judgment Day (1991) – I think most people my age know Arnold as the Terminator. Whether it be the good Terminator or the bad Terminator I think it's his most iconic role. I'm a T2 guy...I think the movie is better and Arnold is cooler.

2. Predator (1987) "Dillon...you son of a bitch." Great performance as the leader of group of rag tag commandos hunting bad guys out in the jungle. A lot of great performances in this one. The film is a blast. I could watch this at any time. I also love how unintelligible Arnold is at points in the movie...I remember watching with subtitles to make sure I hadn't missed anything.

3. Kindergarten Cop (1990) – "It's not a tumor." I've probably not seen this in 20 years but it holds a high nostalgia factor in my mind. At 8 years old this was probably my first Arnold flick. Also, I feel like that ferret for a pet was way ahead of its time.

4. True Lies (1994) - Great Arnold flick. Love the story of the family man being a secret agent. Jamie Lee Curtis and Tom Arnold are amazing as well. Fun fact: I just purchased this DVD from a lady at work for $1. Is this Arnold's funniest movie?

5. Last Action Hero (1993) – An underappreciated film of Arnie's. I just really love the story of the kid going into the world of movies and interacting with the Arnold character. The kid is pretty annoying but the bad guy is dear brother Numpsa from The Golden Child (1986)...great casting.

Arnold Schwarzenegger (L)

1. T2 (1991) - This classic barely nudges out Jingle All the Way (1996) for the top spot…I kid. There is no feasible way to not list this #1. If someone did, I would fight them. Would probably lose, but fight them none the less.

2. Kindergarten Cop (1990) - What a fun movie to watch as a child. Premise you could dig, sorta scary but just the right amount. I wouldn't make eye contact with radio or TV towers for six months after seeing this one.

3. True Lies (1994) - LOVE it. Jamie Lee Curtis was a great partner to the Governator here. This was the kind of action movie the whole family could get behind.

4. End of Days (1999) - When you go back and read the synopsis here, you would bet your life this movie sucked but it was really enjoyable. I was 17 when it came out so my whole life was ridiculous so I could easily get behind Satan visiting New York City in search of a bride. Gabriel Byrne stole the show here.

5. Predator (1987) - Certain movies resonate with guys currently in their mid-30's. I think this and T2 are both on that list with Rambo and 14 Jean-Claude Van Damme movies.

Martin Scorsese (C)
1. The Departed (2006) – DiCaprio, Damon, Nicholson, Marky-Mark, Sheen and Baldwin...what a cast. Putting Dropkick Murphy's on the soundtrack was a great tone setter for the film. Here's a question though...who is the actual main star of the film?
2. Goodfellas (1990) – Ray Liotta at his finest. Luke and I have a healthy ongoing debate as to who has the better movies, Ray or Ben Affleck. I always say Ray's work in Goodfellas outshines Ben's entire career. That's not hyperbole. The one-shot scene where Ray is greeting every person in the Copacabana is iconic.
3. Shutter Island (2010) – Read the book first and really enjoyed it. Saw the film and enjoyed it just as much as the book. A lot of similarities to his Inception character. You never know what's real or not.
4. Casino (1995) – On my first Vegas trip I was scared of being pulled into a side room and my thumbs broken...or driven out to a corn field. I haven't seen this in probably 15 years but I remember really liking it.
5. Michael Jackson's "Bad" Music Video (1985) – Thinking outside the box here...and I've come to realize that I haven't seen as many Scorsese movies as I thought. MJ's third best music video makes the list.

Martin Scorsese (L)

1. Goodfellas (1990) - Big shout out to Casey's favorite actor, Ray Liotta. This movie gets plenty of love but I honestly think it is better than some of those other mob type movies. Also, one of the few mob movies I feel like I could watch again.
2. Gangs of New York (2002) - I saw this in the theaters on Christmas Day. Cinematically, I felt like it was shot in a very unique way. I'm not a big fan of Leo, but I thought Daniel and even Cameron were very good in this film.
3. The Departed (2006) - An all-star cast that deliver the goods. I'm also pretty sure it holds the record for most gunshot wounds to the head in a 90 second period. It was tough seeing one of my favorites, Matt Damon, being the bad guy but was still a great story.
4. Shutter Island (2010) - Not often does the movie do the book justice. I thought this was an exception. I loved this book and was pumped to see it being made into a film. I thought it was creepy and they did it justice in just about every way.
5. Casino (1995) - This one is hard to watch. I'm embarrassed to say this, but I haven't seen very many of his movies. If I have to name five, this is the fifth although I didn't particularly enjoy it as much as everyone else apparently. It also is tough for me since I am in cornfields quite often.

Ridley Scott (C)

1. **Gladiator (2000)** - This movie still gives me chills. Russ Crowe is the best thing ever in this role. This movie is also the reason I want to throat punch Joaquin Phoenix still to this day. Amazingly done film. Killer soundtrack as well. "Father to a murdered son. Husband to a murdered wife. And I will have my vengeance, in this life or the next."

2. **Alien (1979)** – My personal favorite film in the Alien franchise is the original. The alien creature is pretty terrifying and some great practical effects were used. Loved the true horror feel of this one. Great cast and the chest bursting scene is so iconic.

3. **Blade Runner (1982)** - Blade Runner is an acquired taste. When I first saw this movie when I was maybe 10-12, I was beyond bored. When I came back to it in my 20's...I was more impressed. When I watched it again in my 30's...I really enjoyed it. It's art, not a blockbuster film. A great performance from Rutger Hauer really carries the film. Also people that say that Deckard is a Replicant are no friends of mine (Ridley Scott included).

4. **Black Hawk Down (2001)** - Black Hawk Down gives you a glimpse of urban warfare and it terrifies me. The best part of this movie is the bad ass Eric Bana. I was a huge Eric Bana fan for like one year, then I saw more of his resume.

5. **Kingdom of Heaven (2005)** – A solid Scott film rounds out my top five. The film itself was very well made and I loved the Crusades atmosphere. Orlando Bloom was only ok and this movie seemingly went on longer than the Crusades.

Ridley Scott (L)

1. Gladiator (2000) - I am fairly certain the world was my oyster after seeing this. I was pumped and ready to fight a stranger to the death (I'm being facetious). In hind sight, there were glairing historical errors but that wouldn't have mattered to the people I could have killed with a sword.

2. Black Hawk Down (2001) - A raw and gritty film. I liked the way it was filmed and it captured a moment in time that really had been lost to me up until its release. True story...No idea Ridley Scott directed this until researching him for this project.

3. American Gangster (2007) - I don't think it was necessarily God's gift to cinema as some acted when it came out. That said, a phenomenal cast and great story.

4. The Martian (2015) - A more lighthearted effort by Ridley Kingsly Scott (no idea if that is his middle name). Ridley Scott must have dirt on everyone in Hollywood because the guy builds casts more than anyone else. I love the story and it is good every now and then to see everyone make it out ok.

5. Kingdom of Heaven (2005) - I love the location and setting. Obviously, people were a little perplexed by the lack of enormous fighting sequences but it was harder to produce huge budget action films back then. It was a simpler time, heck Orlando Bloom was relevant then so that tells you something.

Will Smith (C)

1. Men in Black (1997) – Tough chore making my top five for Will. I generally like all of his movies so this was not easy. I put MIB at the top due to overall pure entertainment. Had a great family theater experience for this movie.
2. Independence Day (1996) – Actually watched this one with my family in theaters as well. This movie was such a big deal in 1996. Aliens invading earth while Will, Goldblum and President Pullman have to save the day. The most unbelievable thing about this movie was that Harry Connick Jr. played a fighter pilot.
3. Wild Wild West (1999) – Will was a great Jim West. The movie wasn't a big financial success but it's still fun to watch. Great theme song for the movie done by Will and Sisqo.
4. Bad Boys (1995) – This movie was another big deal at the time. Everybody was talking about Bad Boys in 95. Will and Martin Lawrence were a comedic powerhouse. Rumor has it we have another Bad Boys sequel being made...I'll watch it.
5. Suicide Squad (2016) – There is a good reason for SS making the list...felt like a return to old school Will Smith. Deadshot was a fantastic role for Will, made him look strong and let him use his God given talents. Even though I had major issues with the CGI and the villain, I thought this was the best DC movie...until I saw Wonder Woman (2017).

Will Smith (L)

1. Independence Day (1996) - I came to a realization, I really haven't overly enjoyed Will Smith. I almost feel bad saying this because he seems like a swell guy but shouldn't something be higher than Independence Day? Maybe it is Jeff Goldblum...not even crazy Randy Quaid can knock this off of #1.

2. Ali (2001) - I saw this on Christmas Day. I dug the movie and William's dedication to the role. My one beef, and perhaps it was my own fault, I really thought it was a full fledge biopic, not a glimpse into the career. The soundtrack had a great African jam as well that is still floating around my car on a burnt CD from college.

3. Hitch (2005) - Sentimental meaning here. Early on while dating, Allison and I rented this Rom-Com. Not great but holds a place on my list for my admittance above.

4. Bad Boys (1995) - Have to be honest. I don't remember this movie much. I watched it when it was all the rage in junior high and haven't watched it since. It could very well be one of those movies where if I watched it again, it might be #1 or not on the list at all...

5. Men in Black (1997) - I did not see any of the sequels so one could argue how much I really liked this but I do remember enjoying it. Perhaps science fiction just isn't my cup of tea. I am surprised at how some of Will Smith's biggest films haven't come on my radar. I haven't seen Wild Wild West (1999), I Robot (2004), I Am Legend (2007). Although I was greatly depressed one Christmas when I watched Seven Pounds.

Steven Spielberg (C)

1. Jaws (1975) – I'll try not to put this on too many lists but it's had such an influence on my life. I saw this very early in life and was mesmerized/terrified. To this day I'm obsessed with Sharks...like I watch every single shark documentary on Shark Week. I'm also still terrified of open water. There is something so terrifying about a great white lurking under the water. Story + Sharks + Characters = A+ Movie.

2. Jurassic Park (1993) - Saw this movie 3 times in theaters I loved it so much. Michael Crichton (RIP) gets a shout out for writing the source material but Spielberg gets even more credit for bringing JP to life. This movie seemed so real and the CGI was not distracting. "Hold on to your butts."

3. Indiana Jones and The Last Crusade (1989) – My favorite Indy flick. I think I saw Temple of Doom (1984) first then Last Crusade and finally Raiders (1981). I was about seven so naturally I found the Last Crusade the most entertaining. Great performance from Connery and the "obstacle course" Indy goes through is unforgettable. "Choose wisely."

4. Catch Me if You Can (2002) – Incredible film based on a true story about a professional con man. Tom Hanks and Leonardo DiCaprio are fantastic in this movie. They both should have beat Adrian Brody in the Pianist (2002) for the Oscar. Also I love the name Carl Hanratty.

5. Bridge of Spies (2015) – A more recent Spielberg flick that I really enjoyed. Nice mix of drama and humor and I felt like this was Tom's best performance in quite some time. I hope to be able to add Ready Player One (2018) to this list...knock on wood.

Steven Spielberg (L)

1. Saving Private Ryan (1998) - Spielberg's list of movies is crazy. I think there should be a federal mandate that he must be involved with one movie a year. I can't wait until my boys are hold enough to handle this movie. I am already daydreaming about it.

2. Jurassic Park (1993) - I won't lie; I was a little scared to watch this as a kid. For a good chunk of my childhood, this was my favorite movie. What little boy doesn't dream about dinosaurs? Seeing a T-Rex eat a man off of a toilet was quite the site for a youngster. The first movie I remember Jeff Goldblum in as well.

3. Raiders of the Lost Ark (1981) - This movie was so good that 37 years later we are still talking about it. Also it makes me cry because I just did the math to realize it is 37 years old...anyway, how many archeologists did this movie spawn? Indiana Jones was absolutely one of the most iconic characters in cinematic history.

4. Hook (1991) - An amazingly fun movie. Saw this with dad in the theaters. I think it is one of Robin William's best performances. Also how good and diverse is Dustin Hoffman?!?!? Throw in a cute little Julia Roberts and this is a smash hit.

5. Lincoln (2012) - Daniel Day Lewis + Spielberg = Dream Team. Honest Abe in an accurately themed history piece was awesome. I almost stood up and gave a slow clap at the end of the movie.

Denzel Washington (C)

1. Inside Man (2006) – This movie is awesome from the opening song all the way to the end. To be fair Clive Owen is really good but Denzel is even better. He plays the cool Detective so well. "This ain't no bank robbery."

2. Déjà vu (2006) – I'm a big fan of time travel...so naturally I love the theme mixed with Denzel. Love the New Orleans setting. Also, great to see Val Kilmer in a small role. 2006 was a great year for Denzel.

3. Man on Fire (2004) – This is the ultimate bad ass Denzel movie. If you are ever traveling to Mexico make sure you take Denzel with you. Dakota Fanning tries her best to ruin this movie but is unsuccessful.

4. The Pelican Brief (1993) – So yea I already listed this with Julia...but Denzel is just as good in it. I remember my dad really being jazzed up to see this film after reading the Grisham novel. Gray Grantham is a really cool character name as well.

5. Remember the Titans (2000) – "We are the Titans...the mighty mighty Titans!" This movie rules. In fact I've never once come across anyone who ever disliked it. Excellent coaching by Denzel.

Denzel Washington (L)

1. Glory (1989) - Already mentioned but my goodness. The few small tears as he is whipped for punishment still gives me goosebumps. He has done soooo much but this early film of his still resonates with me the most.

2. Training Day (2001) - You know an actor is good when he drops a performance like this. I just couldn't believe my eyes watching Denzel play a bad guy so well. I think he nailed it and opened a lot of people's eyes to how he can play a foil so well.

3. The Pelican Brief (1993) - I recently re-watched this one. It held up and it is great to watch two icons of our era play off of each other. Still enjoy this one like crazy. It's a thinking man's thriller and I like those better than straight action.

4. Remember the Titans (2000) - Sports, emotion and some great Denzel. All ingredients that make a really solid movie. This story about a high school football team came out when I was in high school myself so I think it was especially effective to peeps our age.

5. Inside Man (2006) - Sneaky good film. I feel like this one somehow fell under the radar. I remember seeing this as an intern in South Bend, IN. I really dug it. Still puzzled that so few have seen it let along talk about it.

Living actors (C)

1. Kurt Russell – Here's a true story. I once had a friend ask me what some of my favorite movies were. I threw out about 10 movies including The Thing (1982), Tombstone (1993), Big Trouble in Little China (1986), Tango and Cash (1989) and Escape from New York (1981). And he said to me, "So you're a big Kurt Russell fan". And as I reflected I thought "wow, I guess I am". I'm so happy he is having a late career resurgence.

2. Russell Crowe – Nothing great lately...although I really liked The Nice Guys (2016) but his performances in Gladiator (2000) and LA Confidential (1997) are acting at its finest. Also, love him in 3:10 to Yuma (2007) and Master and Commander (2003). Full disclosure I also really enjoy him singing in Les Miserables (2012)...yea I said it.

3. Eddie Murphy – Whenever I see 80's/90's flicks with Eddie Murphy, it automatically brings a smile to my face. His smile is so damn infectious! I wish Eddie hadn't lost his smile. But never the less...Beverly Hills Cop (1 and 2), The Golden Child (1986), Coming to America (1988), Trading Places (1983), Shrek (2001), the "Do You Remember the Time" music video...what a resume.

4. Denzel Washington – There is just something so cool about Denzel. The man just puts out hits. You want drama? Done it. You want action? Done it. You want Denzel to be funny? Done it. You want Denzel to stop a runaway train? Done it.

5. Michael J Fox – I have to admit his role as Alex P. Keaton is a major factor in my fondness for MJF. But he also made the Back to the Future Trilogy...which is freakin' timeless. Then there's Teen Wolf (1985) which is criminally underrated! Special Mention: Secret of My Success (1987), The Hard Way (1991) and The Frighteners (1996).

Living Actors (L)

1. Tom Hanks. A true testament to Tom. He doesn't put out many movies anymore but his credit list remains immensely deep. Humor, drama and some action. Old Tom has done it all and did it better than anyone.
2. Harrison Ford. His credit list isn't quite as diverse as others on this list, but Star Wars and Indiana Jones titles alone merit contention. Add in his Jack Ryan movies, The Fugitive (1993) and others? No brainer for me.
3. Morgan Freeman. Deeeeeeep list of credits that has had many a hit covering my lifetime.
4. Robert De Niro. One could argue he often plays the same character. That being said, read through his movies. No seriously, read through them right now and convince me he doesn't have a spot on this list.
5. Christian Bale. Maybe a bit of a hot take here. Obviously he might not be the "best guy" but that isn't what we are judging here. The thing I like about Bale, he has his blockbusters but he also picks projects all over the board both in character and budget. Very diverse which I have always respected. Plus he was willing to starve himself for a role…..well done sir.

Living Actresses (C)

1. Sandra Bullock – I've always been a big fan of Sandra. I think she is a great actress and can do it all. She won me over with her early comedic roles but she really is a jack of all trades. Some of my faves: Demolition Man (1993), Speed (1994) and While You Were Sleeping (1995).

2. Salma Hayek – I've had a movie crush on Salma for a long time...it's no secret. But she's not just a pretty face, I really do enjoy her performances. Most notable for me...Wild Wild West (1999) and From Dusk till Dawn (1996).

3. Jennifer Anniston –Jen is mostly remembered for her work in TV but over the last decade she has transitioned her charm to the big screen. While she may not be in the most popular movies I love her humor. Please see Horrible Bosses (2011), We're the Millers (2013) and Just Go with It (2011). If you've already seen them...watch them again.

4. Emily Blunt – I'm going to be blunt (wink) about this one...I love Emily's accent. I think she is a great actress but she's in my Top 5 mostly due to her intoxicating accent. Favorite role...Edge of Tomorrow (2014).

5. Zoe Saldana – Zoe is one the greatest action stars going today. She has had so many great roles and been involved with some big time movies. The Guardians flicks, Avatar (2009), Star Trek series and I recently just noticed her small part in Pirates of the Caribbean (2003). In summary Zoe is awesome.

Living Actresses (L)

1. Julia Roberts. Julia hasn't done much in the last decade but was the belle of the ball in the 1990's as I was growing up. The 90's was an amazing era for film and she nailed many a performance. From top to bottom, her credit list competes with anyone.
2. Natalie Portman. I think Portman is sensational. She has done a bit of everything and even snuck in some great titles like Star Wars and Beautiful Girls (1996) before she was even 20. V for Vendetta (2005) might be my personal favorite performance.
3. Rachel McAdams. The Notebook (2004) holds special in my heart as it was a memorable date fairly early on with Allison and I. Midnight in Paris (2011) showed range. Wedding Crashers (2005) is a classic. Oh and she is a gorgeous lady.
4. Emma Stone. I think she will go down as one of the all-time greats. She has done so much already. Sky is the limit here.
5. Sandra Bullock. I honestly wasn't considering her but then I got to thinking….Speed (1994), Gravity (2013), Crash (2004), The Blindside (2009), A Time to Kill (1996)…Good grief she has had a career!

Movies Directed by a Female (C)

1. Wayne's World (1992) – Penelope Spheeris – One of my all-time favorites. I remember watching this for the first time at my buddy David's birthday party. The Bohemian Rhapsody scene is one of the greatest scenes in cinema history. I quote this movie at least once a day. Rumor has it Penelope and Mike Myers didn't see eye to eye during filming.

2. Fast Times at Ridgemont High (1982) – Amy Heckerling – Watched this for the first time in 2017! I know calm down everyone. I don't know what to say. It just slipped through the cracks. I just never had the desire to see it. I knew of the Spicoli character and judged a book by its cover. I had no idea how amazing the movie was. The opening features an 80's mall shot which set the tone for a great experience. This movie also had a little bit of a dark side to it as well which I was not expecting. Well done Amy, well done.

3. Wonder Woman (2017) – Patty Jenkins – This movie was fantastic and what a great surprise…usually DC puts out less than stellar films. I think Patty deserves a lot the credit, the whole film ties the story of Wonder Woman together nicely. Gal Gadot is the best of the DC new wave heroes. It's not even close.

4. Big (1988) – Penny Marshall – Pre 90's Tom Hanks is one of the greatest things since sliced bread. I like to refer to 80's Tom as the funny years. This is a great story where a 13 year old wishes to grow up and figures out the harsh realities of being an adult. Special mention… Penny also did A League of Their Own (1992).

5. Point Break (1991) – Kathryn Bigelow – Kathryn has put out some hits. Hurt Locker (2008). Zero Dark Thirty (2012). Point Break has to be my favorite though. Swayze is the best part of this movie, though I find just about everyone entertaining…even Gary Busey. "Backoff Warchild, seriously."

Movies Directed by a Female (L)

1. Zero Dark Thirty (2012) - Kathryn Bigelow - My love for this movie is known. Kathryn Bigelow did a great job of making a dialogue heavy movie seem like an action packed thriller. The fact that the story stems from one of America's most shocking moments also sucks you in from the beginning.

2. Wayne's World (1992) - Penelope Spheeris - I think it is one of cinema's saddest unknown stories. Penelope Spheeris and Mike Meyers had a falling out between this and Wayne's World 2. What could have been if she was at the helm of the sequel…..Surely it would have been better

3. A League of Their Own (1992) - Penny Marshall - Penny did some magic with Thomas Hanks on both this and Big (1988). This one will always hold a place in my heart for its ensemble and sports heavy story. I could literally stop typing and watch this movie right now with no problem.

4. Hurt Locker (2008) - Kathryn Bigelow - What is it with Bigelow's fascination with the modern times tension of the Middle East? Regardless, it really worked for her with this along with Zero Dark Thirty. A critically acclaimed movie worth it's praise that many haven't seen.

5. Lost in Translation (2003) - Sofia Coppola - One of the "indie darlings" that met its acclaim. The first time I saw this I remember thinking that Bill Murray was a national treasure. He was strictly a "ha ha" actor for me until this one. Young Scarlett is also good and what a super unique story. Love it.

Movies with a Female Lead (C)

1. Adventures in Babysitting (1987) - A film frequently rented by my family. In my youth I had a healthy crush on Elisabeth Shue. Adventures in Babysitting is just an all-around great film led by Ms. Shue and I can't wait to show my kids this one. Great opening to the film with her dancing/getting ready for her date. "Don't eff with the babysitter."

2. Alien (1979) – This put Sigourney Weaver on the map. She is so good in Alien and Aliens. Alien is my personal favorite film in the Alien franchise. Loved the true horror feel of this one. Great cast and the chest bursting scene is so iconic.

3. Sweet Home Alabama (2002) – Reese Witherspoon at her finest. She should have just stopped making movies after this one. This movie is so charming and its 99% due to Reese. Melanie Smooter is a great character name as well. "Well hells bells, if it ain't Felony Melanie."

4. The Girl with the Dragon Tattoo (2011) – When this was first announced I was hoping they would get Noomi Rapace to revise her role as Lisbeth Salander but after watching this one Rooney Mara was fantastic in her own right. Rooney outshines Daniel Craig greatly in this one. Love the Lisbeth Salander character.

5. Fargo (1996) – Old Marge Gunderson...what a character. Love the evolution of the character throughout the film. At first we are led to believe she is just a silly cop but by the end you realize she is full of wisdom. Great performance by Frances McDormand. "I'm not sure I agree with you a hundred percent on your police work, there, Lou."

Movies with a Female lead (L)

1. Zero Dark Thirty (2012) - I feel like I have fallen back onto this film too often but I must be true to myself. Jessica Chastain is one of my favorites, the genre IS my favorite and it was incredibly well done. This was the first thing that popped in my mind...after torture of course.
2. Bridesmaids (2011) - As far as comedies go, it's a treasure. Huge fan of Kristen Wiig and the whole cast nailed it. One of the best comedies of the modern era. This is darn near Anchorman (2004) level hilarity. So many quotable lines and the breakout of Melissa McCarthy.
3. The Help (2011) - Who was even the lead here? I don't really think it matters as everyone hit a homerun. I didn't even really recognize Jessica Chastain but please reference my love for her in #1. Emma Stone was great and Bryce Howard was not kind. Oh and I think Viola Davis was so good, she won an Oscar.
4. Silence of the Lambs (1991) - If I had to rank my top 100 favorite actresses, Jodie Foster would not be on the list. However, Clarice was awesome in this thriller that still keeps me up at night.
5. Erin Brockovich (2000) - Julia Roberts is one of the best of all time as far as a "leading lady" goes, this was probably her crowning achievement. She was the lone star of this one and didn't need to share the marquee with a male counterpart.

John Candy (C) Bonus

1. The Great Outdoors (1988) – Nostalgic pick. Reminds me of watching movies with my family as a kid. This was a frequent rental from Prestige Video for the Heatons in the 90's. Some great use of raccoons in the film as well.
2. Planes, Trains and Automobiles (1987) – I really miss John Candy. When I watch his movies I am immediately put in a great mood. Even though the film has a sad turn at the end this is one I could watch repeatedly. "I've never seen a guy get picked up by his testicles before."
3. Uncle Buck (1989) - Uncle Buck comes in at #3 with a great performance from John. I recently went to a fund raiser at an elementary school and whilst using the tiny urinals I was reminded of the classic scene of Candy on a knee while peeing in the elementary school bathroom.
4. Delirious (1991) – I love the concept of this film. A magic typewriter where whatever you type comes to fruition...how awesome! Until someone steals your typewriter. Fun little movie.
5. Armed and Dangerous (1986) – Loved this movie as a kid. Another one we watched a lot as a family. Features a young Meg Ryan and Eugene Levy. It's not as good as I once remembered but definitely worth checking out.

John Carpenter Movies (C) Bonus

1. The Thing (1982) – This was a movie I saw at way too young of an age. Which is maybe why I found it so horrifying. I think this is John Carpenter's best film. The tone is perfect and bleak, the practical effects are amazing and the cast is top notch. Kurt Russell rules as Mac. Nice efforts from Keith David and Wilford Brimley as well. This movie is the perfect horror movie from the opening scene of the helicopter chasing the dog to the conclusion. One of my favorite things in life is sitting down with people and showing them this movie for the first time.

2. Big Trouble in Little China (1986) – Another John Carpenter classic. Jack Burton is one of my all-time favorite characters and he some fantastic lines in this. Kurt steals the show but some great performances by Victor Wong (the Grandpa in 3 Ninjas) and James Hong (he is the Asian Samuel L. Jackson, meaning he has been in like 1 million movies). Also for you Sex and the City fans Samantha is in this. If you haven't seen this please take the proper steps to do so. "We really shook the pillars of heaven, didn't we Wang?"

3. Escape from New York (1981) – Quick summary of this film. One of the greatest actors of all time (Kurt). One of the greatest characters of all time (Snake). One of the greatest scores of all time. Not really sure why but it's my ringtone for when my mom calls me. The supporting cast is phenomenal as well, starting with Lee Van Cleef. This movie also has the mood of a lot Carpenter films wrapped up into one. A+ flick.

4. They Live (1988) – This movie is wonderful. Roddy Piper is so damn good in this movie and has one of the best lines in cinema history. The film also features an amazing fight sequence between Piper and Keith David. Unfortunately I think it was Carpenter's last great film. "I have come here to do 2 things..."

5. Prince of Darkness (1987) – This may have been the toughest list to create. Carpenter has probably 8 "A's" in his resume. I could just have easily included The Fog (1980) or Halloween (1978) but when it comes down to it I like Prince of Darkness a little more. The cast is very underrated, no superstars but a lot of folks that frequently collaborate with Carpenter. The film is super creepy and I love the build of the green ooze. Absolutely loved the old mission building used for the film as well. Bonus...you get to see Alice Cooper kill someone with a bicycle.

Antoine Fuqua (C) Bonus

1. King Arthur (2004) - Love the Arthurian Legend and I think this is the best King Arthur movie. I often describe this movie as King Arthur meets Training Day (2001), which speaks to Fuqua's style. We had a buddy who worked at a local theater and he let us come in after hours for a free screening of this film. Tristan was by far my favorite character.
2. The Equalizer (2014) - What could be better than seeing a mild mannered Denzel Washington beat up a bunch of jerks? That's a rhetorical question. This movie is very simple...and awesome! Denzel and Fuqua clearly work well together.
3. Training Day (2001) – Often regarded as Fuqua's best film. I think it's a good film. Denzel is a fantastic crooked cop but Ethan Hawke sucks.
4. The Magnificent Seven (2016) – Pretty solid remake with a good cast. Denzel and Chris Pratt really carry the film. This was a fun date night movie for me, with a high body count. Being a fan of the original is what brought me to the film...that and I generally see anything with Denzel. Ending is somewhat surprising.
5. Shooter (2007) – Good action thriller. One of the better Marky Mark films. I don't like seeing Danny Glover as a bad guy though, doesn't sit well with me.

2. Sports

As lovers of sports, this section was a must have. We both grew up big baseball fans as well as huge World Wrestling Federation (WWF, now WWE) fans so naturally you will find our Top 5 Baseball Movies and our Top 5 Films Featuring a Pro Wrestler. We threw in a few more for fun as well.

(C) = Casey
(L) = Luke

Movies Featuring a Wrestler (C)

1. They Live (1988) – This movie is legit fantastic. Roddy Piper is so damn good in this movie and has one of the best lines in cinema history. The film also features an amazing fight sequence between Piper and Keith David. Also, its John Carpenter folks. "I have come here to do 2 things…"

2. Suburban Commando (1991) – I know this is kind of a cheesy flick, but I won't apologize for loving it. This was in the prime of my youth and I loved Hulk Hogan. It was also cool to see the Undertaker in small role. The bit where he keeps beating up the mime cracks me up to this day.

3. Predator (1987) – Jesse "The Body" Ventura nearly steals the show. He has some larger than life quotes in this film…most of which would never have made the script if made today. His giant machine gun is pretty sweet as well. "I ain't got time to bleed."

4. Furious 7 (2015) – So I name Furious 7 here but really I include the Rock's body of work from all of his Fast and Furious work from 5-8. The Rock is a legit bad ass and has made a successful transition from the ring to Hollywood. I really wanted to put Baywatch (2017) on the list to be timely, but Furious 7 is better.

5. Spider-Man (2002) – The movie is just ok BUT…my all-time favorite guy Macho Man Randy Savage is in this one. If he had a bigger role I might have put it #2. Ohhh Yeaaaaa!

Movies Featuring a Wrestler (L)

1. The Wrestler (2008) - This might be a cop out because it was critically acclaimed which of course is the exact opposite of most movies that feature wrestlers but this spoke to me. Brutally raw and honest look at the life of a down trodden has been star. Lots of wrestler cameos but Earnest "The Cat" Miller as The Ram's foil is memorable.

2. The Princess Bride (1987) - Obvious choice here with the eighth wonder of the world, Andre the Giant. Cards face up....I still can't understand most of his lines but what a film!

3. Rocky 3 (1982) - Another obvious choice but Thunderlips was a catalyst to Hulkamania taking off so it must be on the list.

4. Spider-Man (2002) - The movie was so-so to be honest but my God, Randy Savage as Bone Saw McGraw?!?! I remember thinking that Macho would explode. He was gassed to the gills and his muscularity during this cameo is worthy alone of the #4 spot.

5. Trainwreck (2015) - I specifically excluded the Rock from this list because he has moved beyond "wrestler". I have a feeling that in 10 years time, I could say the same for John Cena. He is quietly putting together good pieces both serious and funny. I remember watching this in the theaters and him just stealing every scene he was in. The sex scene's awkwardness was only outmatched by its hilarity to me.

Baseball Movies (C)

1. Major League (1989) – This is a film I quote on a daily basis. I remember my dad had recorded this onto VHS from HBO back in the day and I freakin' loved it. I played baseball my whole life and I'd like to think I'm funny so this movie was right in my wheelhouse. "You may run like Mays but you hit like shit."

2. Field of Dreams (1989) – This was a big hit in my household. Probably in my dad's top 10 of all time. Costner ruled in this era. And yes I have been to the actual Field of Dreams field in Dyersville IA. "Go the Distance."

3. Little Big League (1994) – This is what I consider to be the best of the "kid baseball" movies. Here's my logic as a 12 year old: It's ridiculous to think a kid could actually play in the majors...but maybe...just maybe they could be the manager. I also love the Ken Griffey Jr cameo where he rips the hearts out of every Twins fan while robbing the game winning homerun.

4. Angels in the Outfield (1994) – It's kind of strange that I chose 2 baseball movies from 89 and 2 from 94. Quite strange. Saw this one in theaters and was immediately hooked. Young Joseph Gordon-Levitt before he was cool. Drives me crazy but my kids refuse to watch this movie with me. Cameos to be noted: both Adrien Brody and Matthew McConaughey play for the Angels.

5. Bull Durham (1988) – Kevin Costner is the king of baseball movies. You have this one, Field of Dreams (1989) and For Love of the Game (1999). How have they not made a movie where he is the Head Coach!? Kevin, I've already started on the script so give me a call if interested. Love seeing Susan Sarandon as the team floozy. "When you speak of me...speak well."

Baseball Movies (L)

1. Field of Dreams (1989) - Not completely baseball centric as it obviously gears toward drama but what a wonder. I think about it almost every time I walk into a corn field and I walk into more corn fields than almost anyone. It also helped spark my interest in the history of baseball and some of the characters the sport has seen.

2. A League of their Own (1992) - One of my top 25 favorites. This was a VHS at my Grandparent's house. I kid you not, I have seen this movie too many times to count. I even bought Allison a Rockford Peaches shirt one time. Classic performance by Tom Hanks.

3. The Sandlot (1993) - What kid who grew up in the 90's doesn't love the Sandlot? The only knock is that it didn't really deal with true baseball (except for the terrible mustached Dodger scene at the end). This is the Mighty Ducks (1992) of baseball and needs to be on the list.

4. Major League (1989) - One of the best comedy sports movies ever if not the best. Great performances, memorable lines and my heavens those poor Indians. The subsequent sequels never were as good but how could they be?

5. Sugar (2008) - I am going way out here by leaving off some great ones like Bull Durham(1988), For the Love of the Game (1999), etc. This Indy film was really well done. It had no stars, had no budget, but really spoke to me. My background in minor league baseball gave me a small inside track on some of the struggles this movie portrays and I really enjoyed that someone made a movie about the topic.

Basketball Movies (C)

1. Teen Wolf (1985) – Grew up on this one. Some awesomely bad basketball action in this one. Great music and montages. Stiles is one of the greatest characters of any film and I love his t-shirts. One thing that always bothered me is that MJF didn't play the championship game as the wolf. What a dummy. Spoiler alert...the Beavers are still victorious. Also terrible officiating...they let that dickhead stand directly under the basket whilst MJF shoots his free throws.

2. Space Jam (1996) – What an odd film but I love it. I feel like if you're going to make a basketball movie you should definitely have Michael Jordan on board. I mean he is easily the greatest basketball player of ALL TIME. Also a great cameo by Bill Murray. Whenever I play pick-up basketball with friends I liken my style of play to that of Bill Murray's in Space Jam.

3. Semi Pro (2008) - More of an underappreciated Will Ferrell movie but I really enjoy it. Jackie Moon is a great character. Woody Harrelson is actually awesome at basketball, so that's fun to see. "If you see a possum try to kill it, it's not a pet."

4. Blue Chips (1994) – I vividly remember making my mom take me to this movie in theaters. I was a pretty big Shaq fan but this movie also featured Penny Hardaway and a nice Larry Bird cameo. I really only remember Nick Nolte being a dirty coach and illegally recruiting players...that's about it. But it was Shaq's first movie so I stand by it being on the list.

5. Hoosiers (1986) – I can't have a list of basketball movies and not include Hoosiers. It's not my favorite movie but it deserves to be on the list. Hackman with one of his best performances and I love Jimmy Chitwood. "I'll make it". Also I'm sure Luke will mention his intramural basketball team in college was named after the rival of the Hoosiers. But what he

won't mention, Luke's powerhouse team of former basketball players barely survived my team of baseball players in the Intramural Championship one year.

Basketball Movies (L)

1. Hoosiers (1986) - I will punch someone in the face and throw them through a trophy case if they argue with this selection. I think I also am drawn to this because these guys were marginal athletes with a sweet jumper, something after my own heart. My intramural team in college even went by the name of the "Hickory Grizzlies". Two time champs bay-bay.

2. Hoop Dreams (1994) - I didn't check the rule book here but I am putting in a documentary. I think this had a role in the fascination with college basketball recruiting. Really humanizes the game and the situation some of these kids have. Powerful stuff.

3. Blue Chips (1994) - Sadly, probably incredibly accurate. I would hate to know how shady the real stuff is going on today. Them getting Penny and Shaq in this movie really got it some appeal back in the day. I will say that seeing Bobby Hurley as an extra in a Indiana uniform though made me throw up in my mouth a little.

4. Semi-Pro (2008) - I am going comedy here. A little too coarse at times but Will Ferrell comedies are magical when they are set to a sports background. Small part for my boy Andy Richter as well!

5. The Air up There (1994) - What a great movie as a kid. Let me digress here...some of you are probably wondering where Space Jam (1996) is. Let me tell you, Michael Jordan...not a fan. I don't know why but I was the only kid in Illinois during the 90's who hated the Bulls. Never saw Space Jam and never will. Kevin Bacon on the other hand is a fine gentlemen whose movies I view regularly.

Football Movies (C)

1. Necessary Roughness (1991) – Scott Bakula + Sinbad + Football = A great time for young Casey. Now that I'm older I appreciate the Kathy Ireland performance as well. I remember creating the Texas State Armadillos on many a college football video game. "Welcome to Foot...ball."

2. Remember the Titans (2000) – Great story. Great cast. Just an all-around fantastic film, I can't wait to show this to my kids when they're a bit older because I love the message. Denzel carries the film no doubt.

3. Any Given Sunday (1999) – Saw this one in theaters so I think it sticks with me because of that (I love going to the movies). This movie was so well casted. Jamie Foxx, Dennis Quaid, LL Cool J, LT, Pacino, Diaz etc. Willie Beamen yackin' on the field is an image I can never forget. Pacino has a great team speech as well.

4. The Program (1993) – Having played High School football in the 90's, this was a must see. I feel like it was every high school football player's favorite film (at the time). I really liked it back then and it's still pretty entertaining to this day. It makes my list because this was such a big deal. Pretty sure this was my buddy Vaughn's favorite flick.

5. The Waterboy (1998) – The Waterboy just brings a smile to my face. It's so dumb but at the same time it's so funny. Also to be noted Bill Cowher, one of the greatest NFL coaches, makes a cameo. "Joe Montana was quarterback you idiot"

Football Movies (L)

1. Rudy (1993) - Let's look past the fact that apparently the real Rudy was a D-bag and the team never supported him like the movie portrays. What a freaking heart warmer this was. Great stuff from Sean Astin. Having spent some time living and working in South Bend also showed me how much this movie resonates with a ton of people. One of the best underdog movies out there.

2. The Program (1993) - How great was this movie as a teenager? I remember seeing this in the theaters thinking that I was a big deal watching a grown up movie like this. I was the world's biggest FSU mark at the time as well so there were some obvious parallels there.

3. Necessary Roughness (1991) - My dad took me to see this. I loved it to the point where although embarrassing, I remember starting a short story the night I got home about me playing football. I was nine so I'm sure it was high class material. Being nine when this came out also shows that this isn't on the list only because Kathy Ireland was in it. I still remember parts of this movie. Will always have a place in my heart.

4. Brian's Song (1971) - I was assigned this movie as project for "American History through Film" in high school. I rented this from Family Video and watched this alone in my room. Darn near needed a full box of Kleenex. Pure emotion.

5. Remember the Titans (2000) - I covered this on the Denzel list but this was a powerful movie that came out in a formative time in my life. I was the exact age of the high school kids being portrayed in the movie.

Other Sports Movies (C)

1. Caddyshack (1980) – One of the greatest "sports" movies of all time. Such a quotable movie. All-star cast, even though I find Danny super annoying. Dangerfield, Murray, Chase and others really made this a comedy classic. That gopher dancing to Kenny Loggins at the end will always stick with me. Also this is my co-worker Brian's favorite flick.

2. Talladega Nights (2007) – Easily the best racing movie. Yea that's right Days of Thunder (1990) fans. I'll admit I enjoy Will and his antics. Some fantastic quotes from this movie, John C Reilly also phenomenal in this one. "So when you say psychosomatic, you mean he could start a fire with his thoughts?"

3. Mighty Ducks (1991) – "Ducks Fly Together." What a great film about hockey, teamwork, personal relationships and former players forced into community service because of DUI's. Didn't this film inspire an actual professional team to be named the Ducks? I think so.

4. BASEketball (1998) - This movie inspired some great games of BASEketball at my friend Andy's house. The movie is hilarious but what a genius move combining baseball and basketball. I quote this movie all the time while playing pick-up basketball.

5. Dodgeball (2004) - A movie about one of my favorite PE activities. I don't want to sound like a braggart but I was awesome at dodgeball. This movie even led to a series of dodgeball leagues popping up at sports facilities and churches. Fun fact: I played on a dodgeball team in a Church League with Luke.

Other Sports Movies (L)

1. Mighty Ducks (1991) - I am sorry but I have to mark out here as a kid. How great was the Mighty Ducks? I am a little disappoint that Charlie Conway grew up to be the type of guy who would steal Joey away from Dawson but still...

2. Rocky 3(1992) - The quintessential Rocky movie. This movie made Dolph Lundgren. If you are only allowed to watch one Rocky movie, this has to be it right? I think Rocky could be used in 2018 to smooth things over with Russia. I think if we drop DVD copies over Moscow, the world would be a better place.

3. The Fighter (2010) - A true story sports movie with a dynamic cast. Christian Bale is a bit of a jerk in real life and the guy he portrayed is a quack but the movie works! Worthy of its praise.

4. Miracle (2004) - Tag from Friends is a great goalie! Who knew!? You could say it is a little cheesy but you know what, the true story is cheesy so deal with it!

5. Happy Gilmore (1996) - One could argue this isn't a true sports movie but if a bazillion golfers have jokingly tried to swing like Happy, then I think it should count. I think this is Sandler's best movie. Tops Billy Madison but just barely. Bob Barker stole the show. What a professional.

Sports Cameos (C)

1. Dan Marino – Ace Ventura: Pet Detective (1994) – Easily the greatest sports cameo. Dan has some fantastic reactions at the end of the movie. "Hey Ace, you got any more of that gum?"

2. Brett Favre – There's Something About Mary (1998) – Not a Favre fan but his minor role left me with a good feeling about this movie. "I'm in town to play the Dolphins you dumbass."

3. Mike Ditka – Kicking and Screaming (2005) – Da Coach with a great film debut. "Hey Juicebox...get me a juicebox." I love that Will Ferrell dressed up in the iconic Bears Sweater.

4. Lebron James – Trainwreck (2015) – Lebron was singlehandedly the funniest person in the movie. John Cena was the second funniest. "No. Don't pay the whole thing, just pay your part. It's better for our friendship. Equals forever."

5. Charles Barkley, Larry Bird, Mugsy Bogues, Patrick Ewing and Shawn Bradley – Space Jam (1996) – Great to see all of Jordan's rivals in this. "I promise I'll never swear again. I'll never get another technical. I'll never trash talk."

Sports Cameo (L)

1. LeBron James – Trainwreck (2015) - Lebron was so good that I honestly almost view this as a non-cameo. This guy stole several scenes and his performance went beyond what most athletes have put out. Lebron loves Downton Abbey, who knew?!?!

2. Brett Favre. There's Something about Mary (1998) - I remember watching this on VHS up in my room and my jaw dropped when ole Brett showed up on screen. This was before the height of internet insider info. A shocking cameo.

3. Mike Tyson. The Hangover (2009) - This probably is the most insane and funny cameo out there. He was even in the trailer and that still didn't blow his scene.

4. Mike Ditka. Kicking and Screaming (2005) - Ditka was the "Juice Guy". A nice little cameo here by Mike. Pleasantly surprised that the humor outpaced the cheesiness of it all.

5. Dan Marino – Ace Ventura (1994) - I honestly don't remember much of what he did but I remember watching it as a kid and being amazed that Dan would agree to be in such a movie. Probably his crowning achievement since he never won that super bowl.

3. At The Movies

A favorite pastime of ours was and still is seeing movies in theaters. Though having young families doesn't always let us get out as often as we like, we still cherish our time "At the Movies". Some highlights you will find: The Top 5 movies Casey and Luke Have Seen in Theaters Together and the Top 5 movies Seen in TheatersWwhile on Vacation. Cheerio!

(C) = Casey
(L) = Luke

Movies Casey and Luke Have Seen Together in Theaters (C)

1. Old School (2003) – This is one of those movies that was way ahead of its time. We saw it with our other buddy Dusty during our college years. This is a classic college movie. Actually I saw this one twice in theaters. "you're my boy Blue."

2. King Arthur (2004) – Love the Arthurian Legend and I think this is the best King Arthur movie. We had a buddy who worked at a local theater and he would let us come in after hours for free screenings. Tristan was by far my favorite character.

3. 3:10 to Yuma (2007) – I'm sucker for a good western and Russell Crowe is fantastic in this. Solid showing from Ben Foster as well. Christian Bale was ok.

4. From Hell (2001) – A Jack the Ripper flick with a gritty feel and this was back when Depp was still entertaining. Never accept grapes from a stranger.

5. Jay and Silent Bob Strike Back (2001) – This movie is hilarious and will probably never find its way on any other list. So many great quotes from this flick and Will Ferrell steals the show as Federal Wildlife Marshal Willenholly.

Movies Casey and Luke Have Seen Together in Theaters (L)

1. Wrongfully Accused (1998) - Don't get me wrong, this isn't a "great" movie but God help me for some reason I remember everything about that fateful day in the late 1990's when we decided to go see this. I still can't hear "Shoot and gut all the animals in the forest" without losing it.
2. Mothman Prophecies (2002) - A special private showing at South County Cinemas made this one special. Also, ...it freaked me out to the point of near pants urination.
3. 3:10 to Yuma (2007) - Nothing necessarily special about the viewing experience like the other ones but my goodness, this film. It is one of my Top 25 movies period.
4. We Were Soldiers (2002) - We saw this together with a big group of high school friends. Pretty sure we all were on the verge of tears and darn near joined the Marine Corps.
5. Scary Movie 2 (2001) - Again it is the memories. This is a terrible movie, I will give anyone that but seeing it on "The Minor League Baseball Tour" with Casey and Vaughn was memorable. "Take my strong hand!!!!"

Best Theater Experiences (C)
1. Pirates of the Caribbean (2003) – Easily my top movie experience. I think it's because I love traveling to Caribbean islands. But this film pulled me into the scenery like no other before. I really felt like I was there. I hadn't even been to Disney and done the ride yet. Love the score as well. "Ya savy?"
2. Batman (1989) – My first ever movie theater experience. This is where it all began. I will never forget my sister spilling the beans telling me we were going to see Batman that night. Then about 20 minutes later my dad came in to explain we were going to the theater to see Batman and if it gets too intense just to cover my eyes. Obviously I did not cover my eyes.
3. Get Smart (2008) – Not a great movie but it was entertaining. The reason this makes the list is because I saw this the day after I married my wife at the theater on the Plaza in KC. I was still on a high and it was the first movie I saw as a married man.
4. 23 (2007) – Another one that wasn't great but the experience was fantastic. Saw this with my buddy Nate down in Fort Myers, FL. We were the only two people in this huge theater. Super creepy movie that was amplified by being alone in the theater. And on top of that, when my buddy went to the bathroom during the previews (amateur move) I was all alone for that creepy doll movie Dead Silence (2007) trailer.
5. Transformers (2007) – I was a huge Transformers cartoon fan in the 80's. I had been wanting this movie since the 90's and in 2007 my dream was coming true. Then I realized those movies you are often most excited about...end up being terrible. I also wasn't a big Shia LaBeouf fan. I went in with very low expectations. I thought the film was fantastic and it flooded me with happy feelings. I will never forget it. "You eying my piece 50 Cent?"

Best Theater Experiences (L)

1. Gettysburg (1993) - This is an incredibly random choice. It wasn't even in many theaters. It was so long ago that back then, movies had an "intermission". I was raised a Civil War buff and when I showed up with Big Al, the audience nearly applauded me. I was 11. The next youngest person was probably my dad. A special memory Dad and I still discuss.

2. The Ring (2002) - The first movie I ever saw with my lovely wife. That alone is "list worthy" but added in is the fact that the movie was super creepy...no brainer!

3. Tombstone (1993) - I saw this with my "babysitter" Mick Walls when I was 11. To be honest, I thought I was so big-time strolling into the theaters with a JHS basketball star watching a rated R movie. My goodness it did not disappoint. Can anyone actually appropriately describe how awesome Tombstone is?

4. Star Wars 3: Revenge of The Sith (2005) - No, this is not even in the top half of Star Wars movies but what I can tell you is that I saw this at midnight dressed up as a Crimson Guard. I mean I had to be the only person in the world to dress up as a Crimson Guard right? I remember just staying in character as much as I could all night. Awkwardly standing in an "on guard" position.

5. The Passion of the Christ (2004) - For reasons mentioned in another list, this was so moving. Saw it with my then girlfriend and dad. Pure emotion and self-reflection after walking out of the theater.

Movies I Saw in Theaters while on Vacation (C)

1. Master and Commander (2003) – Saw this with Luke down in South Padre Island. Love me some Russ Crowe. Fun fact we also saw The Missing (2003) on this same trip.
2. Transformers: Dark of the Moon (2011) – Took this one in on a family vacation to Destin, FL. On the same trip my mom tried to order a Slice at a restaurant even though Slice hasn't been made in conservatively 10 years. Probably the second best Transformer movie.
3. 300 (2006) – Vacation/Spring Baseball Trip on this one. My buddy Nate and I saw this down in Fort Myer's, FL. This was a really cool visual movie and I remember loving it at the time. But I haven't seen it since 2006. The sequel is pretty disappointing in case you were curious.
4. The Mummy (1999) – Saw this at the IMAX Theater in Branson, MO. Branson is a frequent spot for Heaton vacations but this is my favorite movie we've seen while down in Branson. Silver Dollar City rules!
5. The Score (2001) – Luke, our friend Vaughn and I went to see The Score in Davenport, IA while on our "Minor League Baseball Tour". This is one of the greatest vacations I've ever been on. So while the movie was only ok, it will always hold a special place in my heart.

Movies I Saw in Theaters while on Vacation (L)
1. Frozen (2013) - This might be a unique choice here but Allison and I took Kale and our niece Sophia to see this on South Padre Island. Kale had only been our son for a few months through the foster system and this was his first ever theater experience.
2. The Great Gatsby (2013) - It was a very solid movie but when you see the late show in Killarney, Ireland after a wonderful dinner at Maurina's...it stands out.
3. Inception (2010) - Allison and I saw this in Portland, ME. An amazing movie that left us scratching our heads and keeping us up at night. Christopher Nolan is a mad genius. I always eagerly anticipate his movies. Also, this cast! My goodness.
4. Along Came a Spider (2001) - I have vivid memories of seeing this in South Padre Island with my friend Nick. He called the reveal early. Funny story also about this one. We had major issues with our hotel and my mother voiced her displeasure before leaving to go see this. Upon returning, our door to our room was wide open. I slept with one eye open unsure of whether someone was either going to kill me or kidnap me for ransom.
5. Scary Movie 2 (2001) - I have no idea why this makes the list because it was not good, but the silliness of seeing this movie while foraying through Iowa as a 18 year old sticks out. The "Minor League Baseball Tour" has many things that stick out. We also saw The Score (2001) on this trip but for the life of me, this dumb one is the one I always remember.

Worst Movies I saw in the Theater (C)

1. Excess Baggage (1997) – These were my early high school years where all I did was go to the movies on the weekends. All I remember about this movie was how awful Alicia Silverstone was. I blame Aerosmith for getting her into acting.
2. Seven Years in Tibet (1997) – Looking back what was I thinking going to see this? I was a freshman and saw it with my girlfriend at the time. Longest two hours of my life. I'll never forgive you Brad Pitt.
3. Now and Then (1995) – Went with a girl I liked. The movie was so bad I never hung out with her again...just kidding...or am I?
4. Flubber (1997) – I have mixed feelings about listing this one. I love Robin. It just doesn't feel right. But I actually re-watched this not long ago and it's still horrible.
5. Surfs Up (2007) – This is the worst kid's movie I have ever seen...hands down. Lord have mercy. I don't even think penguins are that cute anymore.

Worst Movies I saw in the Theater (L)

1. Problem Child 2 (1991) - I remember begging Dad to take me to see this. I was nine and it was PG-13 so it was quite the accomplishment when he agreed. Even at nine, I remember thinking "I shouldn't be here". It was so dumb and so immature that even at nine, I highbrowed it.

2. The Beach (2000) - Leo is one of the greats but this movie sucked so badly in my opinion. I remember seeing this with friends. Maybe I wasn't paying attention, maybe it was because I had no interest in drug use but my goodness I remember hating this.

3. Captain Corelli's Mandolin (2001) - A high school girlfriend of mine wanted to see this. Not sure what I expected since she picked it out but it was not a "war movie" as I had hoped. I literally remember next to nothing about it other than loathing the fact that I was stuck there watching it.

4. Freddie got Fingered (2001) - Why did I see this? What did I expect? These are serious questions, someone please let me know.

5. Gods and Generals (2003) - This probably isn't deserving but would be wayyyy up there on "most disappointing". My love for history and the Civil War is documented. Gettysburg (1993) is one of my all-time favorites. This second installment was abysmal. While I personally enjoyed parts, it was a major drag with forgettable performances. It was a long winding road to nowhere and the true tragedy is that it was so bad, that all plans for a third installment never materialized.

My Son's Favorite Movies (C) Bonus
1. Home Alone (1990)
2. Flight of the Navigator (1986)
3. Teenage Mutant Ninja Turtles 2: Secret of the Ooze (1991)
4. Space Jam (1996)
5. Scooby Doo Adventures: The Mystery Map (2013)

My Daughter's Favorite Movies (C) Bonus
1. Three Ninjas (1992)
2. Coco (2017)
3. Frozen (2013)
4. Little Mermaid (1989)
5. Leap (2016)

4. Themes

Pretty standard movie categories here. We cover the classic themes...such as our favorite Romantic Comedies, Horror films, Musicals and Westerns. Sure to be a favorite of the purists out there.

(C) = Casey
(L) = Luke

Bond movies (C)

1. Live and Let Die (1973) – Big time controversial statement coming…Roger Moore is my favorite Bond. He's not the best actor of the group but I prefer him as James Bond. Live and Let Die is by far my favorite Bond flick and it's not even close. Not only is it the best Bond movie but it also has the best Bond theme. This movie absolutely screams 1970's and it definitely is dated but I think that adds charm. Jane Seymour as Solitaire, is my top pick as "Bond Girl" as well.

2. GoldenEye (1995) – This was a great time for a Bond resurgence. I was in junior high when the Pierce Brosnan era began. I thought this was a great comeback for the series. Also to be noted, there was a killer Nintendo 64 game with the same title that I spent hours upon hours playing. In fact the game is probably more popular than the movie. Tina Turner with a solid theme.

3. Skyfall (2012) – I don't think Daniel Craig was a good Bond BUT I thought this movie was really good. Loved the mood of the film and the call backs to some of the older films. Adele had a great theme as well.

4. Thunderball (1965) – Here you go you Connery fans. I feel like this is not a popular Bond flick but it's one of my favorites. It's got sharks, underwater fight scenes and Tom Jones on the theme. BOOM!

5. Tomorrow Never Dies (1997) – I've just always really loved this storyline. The mad media mogul who breaks news because he is the one behind it all. So it comes in at #5 due to my enjoyment of the story. Sheryl Crow does the theme which is pretty forgettable.

Bond Movies (L)

1. GoldenEye (1995) - This was my first Bond movie experience. I think Pierce was a very capable Bond although a couple of his films weren't all that spectacular. Let's cut to the chase...we played the heck out of GoldenEye on Nintendo 64. I honestly don't want to know the amount of hours I spent playing that video game.

2. Skyfall (2012) - I think Craig really hit his stride here. Bardem was a great villain and the story was crisp and sharp. I also remember seeing this in the theaters over Christmas with family from Belgium, which is a special memory. Spectre couldn't follow this.

3. Live and Let Die (1973) - One of the few older Bonds that I have seen from start to finish. Dr. Quinn Medicine Women as a gorgeous young lady is something I can really rally behind.

4. The Spy who Loved me (1977) - Another one of the oldies that I have seen. I think if you see this as a kid, it immediately sticks out because of Jaws and that, honestly is why I remember this one distinctly.

5. Casino Royale (2006) - This was very solid. I think it deserves a spot because it made everyone who likes movies rest a bit easier. It was really hard to imagine Daniel Craig being a serviceable Bond. I remember blasting the decision and thinking it was terrible. This was an excellent first step and has led to a couple really good movies.

Disney Cartoon Movies (C)

1. Aladdin (1992) – Whenever someone asks me my favorite Disney cartoon I never even hesitate. I've just always loved Aladdin, it was right in 10 year old Casey's wheelhouse. The movie features great tunes but more importantly Robin Williams as the freakin' Genie.
2. Lion King (1994) – Maybe the best soundtrack song for song of any Disney film. Remember when Jonathan Taylor Thomas was relevant?
3. The Great Mouse Detective (1986) – A very underrated Disney flick. You gotta appreciate a Sherlock Holmes themed cartoon. And I love the way that adorable little Scottish mouse pronounces the name "Toby".
4. Hercules (1997) – Just a very enjoyable flick mixed with Michael Bolton's "I Will Go the Distance". Bonus points for including Danny DeVito.
5. Mulan (1998) – for 2 reasons...1) Eddie Murphy 2) "I'll Make a Man Out of You" by Donnie Osmond. No further questions your Honor.

Disney Cartoon Movies (L)

1. Aladdin (1992) - Robin Williams immediately comes to mind. One of the few Disney movies I saw in the theaters and I still remember it as a 35 year old.

2. Beauty and the Beast (1991) - Even with a very solid live action big budget remake, the original still resonates with me. My wife's favorite and it carries a lot of sentiment with me.

3. The Lion King (1994) - The soundtrack alone is worthy of this placement. Great story that is timeless and emotionally charged.

4. Peter Pan (1953) - Another movie that my wife adores. I remember telling her that I never saw it early on in our relationship. She nearly dumped me. I have watched it many times since. Watching her watch the movie is what makes it memorable to me. She is six all over again...

5. Little Mermaid (1989) - I gotta be honest. I was never a huge cartoon guy and didn't watch much Disney. Only later in life did I learn to sing along with "Kiss the Girl". That is why this is #5.

Horror Movies (C)

1. The Thing (1982) – This was a movie I saw at way too young of an age. Which is maybe why I found it so horrifying. I think this is John Carpenter's best film. The tone is perfect and bleak, the practical effects are amazing and the cast is top notch. Kurt Russell rules as Mac. Great work from Keith David and Wilford Brimley as well. This movie is the perfect horror movie from the opening scene of the helicopter chasing the dog to the conclusion. One of my favorite things in life is sitting down with people and showing them this movie for the first time.

2. Cabin in the Woods (2011) – Not your typical horror movie by any means. This is more of a horror/comedy and it is fantastic. It's not at all what I was expecting from the trailer. It appears to be your typical horror flick with a group of teens staying in a Cabin in the Woods…but it is so much more. One of the more surprisingly fantastic films of the 2000's.

3. Friday the 13th (1980) – I'm really listing the entire Friday the 13th series. In elementary school I would go over to my buddy Adam's house for scary movies. And for whatever reason we ended up watching these a lot. The Jason character has always been my favorite over Freddy and Michael Myers…but probably because I was exposed to him first. Bonus…the first film in the series has Kevin Bacon.

4. Halloween III: Season of the Witch (1980) – Season of the witch is my favorite of the series even without Michael Meyers. I would argue that Conal Cochran is way more evil than Meyers. This dude wants to kill every kid in the world. Also the Silver Shamrock jingle is phenomenal. If you don't like this movie I will fight you…just kidding (I'm not kidding).

5. Return of the Living Dead (1985) – "Brains!" What a fun movie experience. This is not your typical zombie flick. It's funny, it's dark and the characters are so

different that what I was expecting. I love these characters so much even though they all seem a bit shady. The zombies themselves are a bit unique and of course there's the Tar-Man.

Horror Movies (L)

1. The Shining (1980) - Is this "horror", "scary", or a "thriller"? I don't know and am not sure I care. It was creepy as heck and sticks with you. Very few movies leave you guessing for decades after a release. It was great at slowly building anticipation. The ending was effective although science has proven that no one alive knows what the heck the ending was all about. A classic.

2. The Ring (2002) - I like my scary movies more ghost centric as opposed to horrific gory killing. The Ring checked all the boxes for me. A spooky mind bender with eerie moments and jump out of your seat thrills. Was also the first movie I saw with my wife in the theaters so that counts for something.

3. The Blair Witch Project (1999) - I will get flack for this but I bought into the buzz on this. Was it real? A documentary? Based on real events? Just a general WTH time for scary movies. I also don't get motion sickness so I had that going for me.

4. Candyman (1992) - Don't ask me why but in junior high, this was my go to "scary movie". This was the one we rented when someone wanted to watch a scary flick for the first time. I still probably wouldn't say Candyman three times in a mirror, in fact I just tried to come up with a way to type about this movie without mentioning that specific word.

5. Saw (2004) - Troubling. I will never watch another Saw movie even though I believe Saw 48: That one guy who was dead isn't dead is in post-production. I don't like grotesque killing sequences so this was out of my comfort zone. In fact I am not sure that I liked it at all.

Musicals (C)
1. Moulin Rouge (2001) - Saw this one twice in theaters. The story is solid but the music moves me. The Elephant Love Medley gets me jacked up. Hats off to Ewan McGregor for actually singing.
2. Chitty Chitty Bang Bang (1968) – Dick Van Freaking Dyke. I feel like that's all I really need to say about this one. This is far less known than Mary Poppins (1964)...but its way better. Every song is amazing...that's right every single one. I must give credit to my wife for showing this one to me.
3. Little Shop of Horrors (1986) – A great mix of music, cast and giant human-eating plants. Seriously though this movie is fantastic. A gem on the Rick Moranis resume.
4. Rent (2005) – I love this soundtrack and I've even seen the live production (not Broadway). Again credit goes to my wife for exposing me to this one. I can remember many a road trip while jamming out to the Rent soundtrack. Also to be noted I saw this in theaters with my wife and sister and 50 other women. At one point the entire theater broke out into hysterical crying...except for me of course.
5. Les Miserables (2012) – I like the music and I like the French Revolution story...but what I love most is the singing of Russell Crowe. I'm telling you its hypnotic. Like I know that he is not a good singer but I can't stop listening to him sing. It's the weirdest thing. I truly enjoy it.

Musicals (L)

1. Grease (1978) - We had this on VHS and I am pretty sure my sister Angela watched it 263 times. You can't really help but be drawn in by the music. Olivia Newton John was sensational and no wonder she was an icon of the era after this. Is it physically possible to see this and not sing along? I don't think so.

2. Wizard of Oz (1939) - Another timeless classic that I grew up watching over and over. This story has woven itself into the fabric of society. I just took my oldest son to see a performance of this in 2017 and it was awesome. The wizardry of this movie (see what I did there?) will never dissipate.

3. The Sound of Music (1965) - It is becoming clear that the Worrell family owned three musicals on VHS in the late 1980's. We didn't have cable so I pretty much could watch the news or one of these top three musicals. Only later in life did I really grasp the story of this one. It only made it better.

4. Walk the Line (2005) - Joaquin Phoenix is weirder than an old cat lady but his performance along with Miss Witherspoon was really something to behold. I was applauding their talent throughout the movie.

5. Sweeny Todd (2007) - Allison and I watched a performance at a local community theater in Memphis, Tennessee back in 2008. That is right, that's a random story. It inspired us to watch the Johnny Depp movie that had recently come out. I kid you not, I am still singing the main song. It has been in my head for nine years now.

Pixar Movies (C)

1. Toy Story (1995) - Sentimental pick. I may have been a little too old for this when it came out but that didn't stop me from loving it one bit. I've always loved the idea of toys coming to life. It's such a great concept and Pixar really nailed it. Side note: Have y'all read *Indian in the Cupboard*?

2. Moana (2016) – If ya smell what Maui is cooking...that's a wrestling reference that I'm sure is lost upon most of you. All around good flick. Great soundtrack, good story and it features Dwayne "the Rock" Johnson. The Rock also sings a fantastic song in this movie. So all I can say for the recommendation...is you're welcome!

3. Coco (2017) - What an incredible story. Pixar hit another homerun with this story surrounding Miguel and his journey to the Land of the Dead. Such a fun flick, with some great imagery and music but be warned...some big time emotional scenes.

4. Monsters Inc. (2001) – Saw this in theaters in my high school years. My girlfriend at the time and I were legitimately the only ones in the theater without a child...still loved it. Probably a red flag on my maturity level though.

5. The Incredibles (2003) – Had a great time watching this at my uncle's sister's house in Sydney, Australia. Did you follow all of that? Pretty entertaining flick heightened by being in a super cool city.

Pixar Movies (L)

1. Toy Story (1995) - The one that changed the animated/kids game forever. I went to see this with a group as a junior high student. I couldn't fathom going to see a "cartoon" in the theater but the girl I liked was going so my hands were tied…..I left having to undersell how much I loved it.

2. Cars (2006) -They have never been able to replicate Lighting McQueen though they have tried many a time. A great movie for boys which is good since I will most likely have to watch this another 20 times in my life.

3. Finding Nemo (2003) - By this time Pixar was doing so well that even as a college student, it was perfectly expectable to watch the movies. Ellen stole the show in a huge way here. Fishes everywhere haven't been seen the same since.

4. Brave (2012) - We took our niece to this movie so it holds a special place in my heart. I also love Europe and geography so it had me with the whole Scottish-centric storyline as well. When I watch this movie, I also speak in a poorly done Scottish accent for 48 hours after viewing.

5. Planes (2013) - It is what it is, a follow up on the success of "Cars". I am still waiting for "Boats" and "Lawn Mowers" to hit theaters. None the less, it is a solid film with a lot of good life lessons for kids tucked away in a fun story. My youngest also cutely refers to the star as "Dusty Crop Hop Hop"

Romantic Comedies (C)

1. Sweet Home Alabama (2002) – Factual statement: this is THE BEST romantic comedy in the universe. I don't feel I even need to defend that statement. It's a great plot, it's funny, it's sad, it's gotta little bit of romance...it's gotta a baby in bar. What more do you need? Lightning sculptures? Yea it's totally got that as well. Reese should have retired after making this movie because she reached the pinnacle.

2. The Wedding Singer (1998) – Sandler still in his prime and one of the few Drew Berrymore movies I enjoy. This is one movie I could literally watch anytime. "Julia Gulia. That's funny."

3. Love Actually (2003) – One of my wife's favorite flicks and for the longest time I pretended to put up with it but then I quit lying to myself. This movie is great. Love all the merging storylines. Even though that kid with the crush is beyond obnoxious, I'd still put this at #3. "I feel it in my fingers, I feel it in my toes."

4. How to Lose a Guy in 10 Days (2003) – Another one I saw in theaters and really enjoyed. McConaughey is almost in my top 5 actors, he and Hudson have tremendous chemistry. Was good to see Lilith from Cheers in this as well.

5. My Best Friend's Wedding (1997) – This makes the list only due to the dinner scene where they break into song. I Say a Little Prayer for you! Genius. Back when Cameron Diaz was tolerable as well. Julia Roberts was a real jerk in this movie.

Romantic Comedies (L)

1. 500 Days of summer (2009) - One of the best movies of the last 10 years. That isn't a typo. Incredibly unique and insanely funny to me. Joseph Gordon Levitt is totally underrated in about everything he does. The soundtrack was spot on. There isn't one thing I don't like about this movie.

2. You've Got Mail (1998) - Not only is this featuring the dynamic duo of Hanks and Ryan but it is easily my wife's favorite movie. I have seen this with her many a time. If there is a chance she reads this publication and doesn't see this listed, I might actually be in grave danger.

3. Sleepless in Seattle (1993) - Back to back for the power couple of "Rom Coms"! What a streak it was for those two. I feel like any American male can unashamedly say they enjoyed Sleepless in Seattle. Even those knuckleheads who feel like it is emasculating to like romantic comedies can get behind this.

4. Just Married (2003) - I am not a huge Ashton fan and RIP Brittany Murphy. I saw this with Allison when we first started dating. I thought it was great. All these years later I am a really big geography and European travel nerd so it is a gift that keeps on giving!

5. Where the Heart Is (2000) - I saw this with a high school girlfriend. I remember going in thinking that it was nice of me to let her pick what we were seeing but after it was over, I remember thinking "Holy Crap, that was pretty good!" One of my early experiences with Natalie Portman who I am a big fan of. Novalee Nation is a character name I will never forget and Ashley Judd put in a good performance as well.

Saddest Movies (C)

1. Empire of the Sun (1987) – I have no idea why we sat down as a family to watch this. I was young when I first saw this and I vividly remember the hardships facing young Christian Bale. The scene where he is separated from his mother tore my heart out. The main theme is absolutely beautiful. In fact I had it on a mixed CD from my college years.
2. The Land Before Time (1988) – I was six and couldn't handle this one. I remember watching this alone in my basement with tears in my eyes. I ended up stopping the movie because it was "boring" but I think my parents were on to me.
3. The Curious Case of Benjamin Button (2008) – This is a great story. They took a great concept and delivered. But it's so depressing when you realize Brad and Cate's relationship days are numbered. Also to be noted my wife called this movie "emotionally mute" after I nearly cried.
4. UP (2009) – I couldn't even get past the first ten minutes when I watched this for the first time. You see the couple lose their baby and then the wife's eventual death. I was questioning this being a kid's movie for sure.
5. The Notebook (2004) – I have to admit this is a great story. Gosling and McAdams really deliver. The ending where they die together MAY have brought a tear to my eye…only maybe though. Saw this one in the weirdest movie theater of all time…I think it was a converted barn theater.

Saddest Movies (L)

1. The Passion of the Christ (2004) - This might seem like an odd choice but I have never been more emotionally affected by a movie. I grew up going to church and am a man of faith today. I have heard about Christ dying for my sins but SEEING it was brutal. I remember leaving the theater thinking that I would watch this movie every Easter but I haven't watched it sense. Terribly sad to watch.

2. Seven Pounds (2008) - True story. For a long time my family would see a movie on Christmas day in the theaters. God only knows why we decided to see this. So depressingly sad that I seriously didn't feel like opening presents that day.

3. The Time Traveler's Wife (2009) - Allison and I watched this soon after her mother passed away. Terrible decision. Being heartbroken is one thing, watching that sweet angel Rachel McAdams being heartbroken was an additional load I couldn't bear.

4. Steel Magnolias (1989) - I'm gonna cut you straight. I don't remember the plot and I don't recall ever seeing this from start to finish but I jumped in on my older sister watching this movie when I was a wee little boy. It was the first time where I had that sudden realization, "Crap they are going to kill this girl!!!" Until that moment, I thought all movies ended happily.

5. The Green Mile (1999) - Good gravy where do I begin. I don't remember the second half of 1999 and I blame that on my depressive state (along with the widespread panic of Y2K) because of this movie. I remember thinking, 'What a great movie....I never want to see it again". 17 years and counting without a re-watch.

Space Movies (C)

1. Alien (1979) – In space no one can hear you scream. What a perfect tag line. Awesome space horror flick. Sigourney Weaver's best movie and a truly terrifying space movie.

2. Apollo 13 (1995) – Here's a more historical look at space. Amazing cast led by Tom Hanks. Every time I hear "Spirit in the Sky" I think of this movie.

3. The Last Starfighter (1984) – Sure it's kind of a Star Wars (1977) rip off...but the nostalgia factor is strong with this one. I remember watching this at my cousin Ryan's house as kids. In fact until recently I didn't even know the name of the film. I just always referenced it as the movie I watched at Ryan's house. Watch out for the Death Blossom.

4. Interstellar (2014) – A Christopher Nolan space joint. A cool story of humanity's survival and a worm hole. McConaughey is pretty good in this as was Jessica Chastain. Overall pretty enjoyable even though I couldn't understand a damn word Michael Caine said. There is a scene where McConaughey watches messages from his kids that are several years old and it's so freaking emotional. It killed me knowing he lost time with his kids. Powerful.

5. Europa Report (2013) – This was a cool low budget space movie I watched on Netflix one day. A team of astronauts are searching for alien life on Jupiter's biggest moon. I feel like it's not well known so I won't spoil it. But go check it out.

Space Movies (L)

1. Apollo 13 (1995) - This is "THE" space movie to me. The cast is stupidly good. Captured America accurately in a super formative time and the story was impeccable because it was true. Tom Hanks hit a home run here. A movie I can start watching at any moment.

2. Interstellar (2014) - I love the "What the heck?" type space movies and this fit the bill. Christopher Nolan is on a helluva streak. Even that bookcase scene can't ruin it for me. Jessica Chastain was also in it and I express my love for her in other lists.

3. Contact (1997) - It is becoming clear that Mathew McConaughey and space is a winning combination for me. Super underrated movie that I list elsewhere. I thought the ending was a nice touch that didn't get crazy but proved our heroes to be true.

4. Avatar (2009) – The pageantry of the movie is something else. I think James Cameron is a pretty full of himself but you got to give him props here. It was unlike anything before it or since. Heck, they even devoted part of Disney's Animal Kingdom to it.

5. Close Encounters of the 3rd kind (1977) - I stumbled upon this movie when I was a kid flipping the channels. I was scared of the dark for three years after that. I never want to watch it again.

Super Hero Movies (C)

1. Batman (1989) - Best Batman movie and Keaton is the best Batman...no brainer. Nicholson is the better Joker in my book but I'll admit Ledger was pretty amazing as well. "Ever dance with the devil in the pale moon light?" Fun Fact: this was the first movie I ever saw in a movie theater.

2. Iron Man (2008) – The original Iron Man was great. Felt like the return of Robert Downey Jr. He's such a great wise cracking protagonist. This also paved the way for the Marvel Universe. Had Iron Man not been such a hit we never would have had 723 Superheroes movies. Also, the sequels are garbage.

3. Avengers (2012) – Great concept...all the superheroes teaming up together for one movie? Well played. Saw this in theaters and I'll never forget laughing out loud when Hulk starts whipping Loki around like a rag doll.

4. Guardians of the Galaxy 2 (2017) – Guardians #1 was good, but I liked #2 better. I love the emotion of this movie! Maybe it's because I am a father myself, but I really dug the father/son story. It really hit me in the feels. Another killer soundtrack. It was also great to see that old-school Dairy Queen at the beginning. "I'm Marry Poppins y'all."

5. Batman (1966) – Grew up on this movie. This was one we rented a lot and watched on TV quite a bit. The tone of the film works perfectly for me. I quote this one a lot and rarely does anyone know what the hell I'm talking about.

Super Hero Movies (L)

1. The Dark Knight (2008) - I think this was the most well done and polished super hero movie. I feel this upped the bar in a big way for super hero movies moving forward. I mention it in another list but Heath Ledger's Joker??? Name me one better performance as a villain. I feel the need to come clean and admit that super hero movies aren't my thing. I don't think I have seen one in the last six years so judge my list accordingly.

2. X-Men (2000) - Not X-Men: Origins (2009). Not X-Men: Days of Future Past (2014). Not X-Men: The 31st one in the last 5 years. The first big hero movie in 2000. I was in a comic book phase when I was younger and read tons of X-Men. I remember thinking back then how cool it would be if they would make a really huge X-Men movie. Low and behold, my dream came true albeit about seven years later.

3. The Dark Knight Rises (2012) - I really, really like Christopher Nolan. I could have lived without Anne Hathaway but hey my boy Jospeh Gordon-Levitt showed up! I saw this while on vacation in Nashville in a huge theater. This was a film to see for sure with a big theater experience.

4. Spider-Man (2002) - This might be one of few movies in which I actually enjoy Toby Maguire. I enjoy films that get the ball rolling. This along with the Batman revamps a few years later is my niche.

5. Batman (1989) – The original will always hold a special place in moviegoer history. Michael Keaton was great and Jack Nicholson brought his skill and credentials along as well. Unfortunately, Batman Returns (1992) belongs on another list...

Movies Featuring Time Travel (C)

1. Back to the Future 1 and 2 (1985/1989) – A bit of a cheat listing two movies so deal with it. These are the quintessential time travel movies. In the first we get to go back in time and in the second we see the future...and that sweet 80's café. The third film was only ok but you do get to see the Wild West.

2. Hot Tub Time Machine (2010) – Went to see this in theaters with basically no expectations. This is probably my top comedy in the last 10 years. Rob Cordry is hilarious and John Cusack doesn't ruin it. If you know me I love all things 80's, so this movie is right up my alley. I like to pretend the sequel doesn't exist.

3. Déjà vu (2006) – I'm a big fan of time travel (obviously or I wouldn't have chosen this category)...so naturally I love the theme mixed with Denzel. A very unique spin on time travel. Love the New Orleans setting. Also great to see Val Kilmer in a small role.

4. Flight of the Navigator (1986) – A frequently watched film from my youth. Showed my kids this for the first time recently and they loved it. I remember being so jealous as a kid when the main character is staying at the NASA facility and he gets all those GI Joe and Transformers toys. You get some good time travel and the voice of Peewee Herman...bonus!

5. Bill and Ted's Excellent Adventure (1989) – Remember when phone booths were a thing? How would Bill and Ted travel back in time in 2018? I remember really liking this film back in the day...I watched it again not long ago and it's still pretty fun. Fun fact: "Dude" is said 70 times.

Movies Featuring Time Travel (L)

1. Back to the Future (1985) - This category is really unfair. Marty McFly and Doc Brown will from here on dominate...
2. Back to the Future 2 (1989) - See #1
3. Back to the Future 3 (1990) - The whole concept of this trilogy was great. Done in a dramatic yet humorous way that can placate to literally any demographic. One of the iconic films of this era right? The amazing thing is that it plays so well in modern times. My sons will soon watch these. They will love it and have no idea that it is nearly as old as their Dad.
4. Looper (2012) - I think this one snuck under the radar. Featuring a legend in Bruce Willis. A diverse modern actor in Joseph Gordon-Levitt. The beauty of Emily Blunt. An amazing touch to make Joseph Gordon-Levitt look like a young Bruce Willis. The story was super unique and thought provoking.
5. Midnight in Paris (2011) - Not your typical time traveling movie, but hear me out. Paris, one of my favorite cities in the world beautifully filmed on location. Outstanding cast with Owen Wilson and Rachel McAdams in the lead. I am not a huge fan of Woody Allen but my goodness this was a really good movie and it wove in historical time traveling really well.

War Movies (C)

1. The Dirty Dozen (1967) – What a great storyline. This is like the original Suicide Squad (2016) without terrible CGI. A maverick Army leader trains a dozen criminals/murders for a top secret mission sure to fail. I was hooked on this one growing up.

2. Kelly's Heroes (1970) – This was one of my dad's favorites...so naturally I love it too. One of the few Eastwood performances I enjoy. A group of soldiers go off script behind enemy lines to find some secret Nazi gold. Weird that Telly Savalas is in my top two films.

3. American Sniper (2014) – Speaking of Eastwood, I think he sucks as a director but this film was amazing. It's a good mix of story and intense action. Bradley Cooper should have received an Oscar. I've never left the theater in such a sobering mood.

4. Glory (1989) – The best Civil War movie is one about the 54th Massachusetts, the first all Black regimen in American history. Denzel and Morgan Freeman deliver amazing performances and really motivated me to be a better person.

5. Black Hawk Down (2001) – Black Hawk Down gives you a glimpse of urban warfare and it terrifies me. The best part of this movie is the bad ass Eric Bana. I was a huge Eric Bana fan for like one year, then I saw more of his resume.

War Movies (L)

1. Gettysburg (1993) – My love for this movie is well documented across many of these lists. Not sure how a low budget film got so many stars. Look past the terrible cheap wigs and beard pieces here. You won't get glitz and glamour in special effects but you'll get a true description on the proceedings of the most important battle of the Civil War.

2. Saving Private Ryan (1998) – Amazing cast, amazing story and cry out loud drama. Is this the pinnacle of both Ed Burns and Barry Pepper? The opening scene alone would get this on the list.

3. Zero Dark Thirty (2012) – Not the type of "War" movie one thinks of but holy-moly do I love this movie about the "War on Terror" and tracking down Bin Laden. Suspenseful and insightful and the lovely Jessica Chastain freaking dominated this role.

4. Glory (1989) - Another repeat offender on my lists. Everything Luke Worrell could want in a war movie. Civil War, cast, storytelling and sob worthy emotion.

5. The Dirty Dozen (1967) - I was raised to respect others, love the St. Louis Cardinals and acknowledge the greatness of the Dirty Dozen. No it isn't historically accurate at all but I think every boy grows up wanting to know what their father's favorite movie was. Dad led me to the Dirty Dozen and I have seen it nearly a dozen times. Oh the irony.

Westerns not Starring John Wayne (C)

1. Tombstone (1993) – Tombstone is always in the rotation for my all-time favorite film. Kurt Russell is a good Wyatt, but Val Kilmer steals the show. It's a shame Kilmer didn't win an Oscar for his role as Doc Holliday. At least Val won the MTV Movie Award for Best Male Performance. A lot of other good performances as well but you get the idea.

2. 3:10 to Yuma (2007) – I'm sucker a for a good western and they just don't make them much anymore. Russell Crowe is fantastic in this. Solid showing from Ben Foster as well. Christian Bale was ok.

3. Magnificent Seven (1960) - Great film with a killer main score. Well I guess it's great if you're into westerns. This film features a phenomenal cast: Yul Brynner, Steve McQueen, Charles Bronson and James Coburn. It's also fun to watch knowing Yul and Steve hated each other during filming. The 2016 remake with Denzel and Chris Pratt was respectable.

4. Blazing Saddles (1974) – The story goes that John Wayne was offered the Gene Wilder role...thank goodness he turned it down. No way could he pull off the wacky character. This was an eye opening movie the first time I watched it. Still blows my mind that Cleavon Little didn't become a star...he was good in this. "Candygram for Mongo."

5. True Grit (2010) - At first a John Wayne remake seemed sacrilegious but then I saw the film and loved it. Only "The Dude" could pull off "The Duke". Well done film. I like Matt Damon in this as well.

Westerns not Starring John Wayne (L)

1. Tombstone (1993) - Freaking money. This has popped up on several of my lists. One of the top 15 movies of all time. There is literally nothing better than Val Kilmer as Doc Holliday. Parts of this movie are engrained in my memory. Don't sleep on Stephen Lang's performance. Sensational.

2. 3:10 to Yuma (2007) - I saw this in the theater with Sir Casey Heaton (he was recently knighted). Love everything about it. Wonderful classical western story. Bale and Crowe might be jerks in real life but I don't care, darn it. Rent this movie!

3. The Assassination of Jesse James by the Coward Robert Ford (2007) - This movie was so different. A great western in a time where they aren't made anymore. Casey Affleck was really good here and the whole cast was well constructed. It also fascinated me to research the real Jesse James. I love it when movies spark historical curiosity and this movie did that.

4. Silverado (1985) - Another great cast ensemble. One of the first westerns I really remember watching when I got a bit older. I like the misfit toy make-up of the story. It goes perfectly with what a western should be.

5. Open Range (2003) - I think this is a sleeper western. No, it isn't as good as some of its recent contemporaries but Kevin Costner was really good. Robert Duvall back in the saddle and in a western also made this memorable. Let's also give it up for Annette Bening who added a lot.

Best Sequels (C)

1. Beverly Hills Cop 2 (1987) – Just as funny as the original. Eddie is pure gold. They assembled basically the same cast with the addition of Brigitte Nielsen and a Chris Rock cameo. Eddie could do no wrong in the 80's. "My name is Johnny Wishbone and I am psychic from the island of St. Croix."

2. Back to the Future 2 (1989) – Arguably the best film trilogy of all time. This one is just as good as the original for me. I like that they actually go into the future this time. I feel like adding Elisabeth Shue to a cast can only improve matters as well. The hover board has become so iconic as well, people are still trying to create one. I wish there was actually an 80's cafe.

3. Terminator 2 (1991) – T2 is actually better than the original. And don't get it twisted I really like the first one. I loved Arnold being the bad ass in the first one but man I think he is even better as the good terminator in T2. Another highlight is the T-1000, such a great villain, he felt unstoppable at times. One minor complaint is Edward Furlong...enough said. Also to be noted, Bobby Budnick from "Salute Your Shorts" has a small part.

4. Ace Ventura When Nature Calls (1995) – This movie rules. Not quite as funny as the original but almost. My sister and I used to quote this movie all the time. In fact back in the days of the scrolling marquee screensavers we had "Bumblebee Tuna" scrolling across. "Let me guess. White Devil, White Devil."

5. Guardians of the Galaxy 2 (2017) – Another instance where I liked it better than the original. I love the emotion of this movie! Maybe it's because I am a father myself, but I really dug the father/son story. It really hit me in the feels. Another killer soundtrack. It was also great to see that old school Dairy Queen at the beginning.

Best Sequels (L)
1. The Empire Strikes Back (1980) - Do I really have to go into depth? This villain butt kicking really set the tone for the whole series that still goes on today. This solidified Star Wars into the billion dollar brand it is today.
2. The Bourne Ultimatum (2007) - This was the third in the series and easily my favorite. I adore this series so that first sentence says a lot. It was a great movie experience and is one of the few films where I immediately bought the DVD upon its release.
3. Terminator 2 (1991) - Can anyone actually recall seeing Terminator 1? I couldn't tell you the first thing about it. I am willing to bet a vast majority of others are in the same boat. This franchise has tried several times since with limited success. This installment can't be topped.
4. Sister Act 2 (1993) - This is off the grid. I will literally punch anyone in the face who says Sister Act is better than Sister Act 2 (Just kidding, I won't hit you but will silently judge). Both VHS tapes resided at my Grandparent's farm. Sister Act 2 was watched repeatedly while the original collected dust. So much better.
5. The Dark Knight (2008) - Batman Begins (2005) was solid but this one, largely thanks to Heath Ledger, was quite the experience. Christopher Nolan delivered. Heath Ledger wowed. Christian Bale's voice was tolerated and this was a huge success.

Worst Sequels (C)

1. Now You See Me 2 (2016) – What a piece of crap this movie was. The first was so entertaining. Even adding Harry Potter to the film couldn't help it. Real snooze fest.
2. Hot Tub Time Machine 2 (2015) If you know me at all, you'll know Hot Tub Time Machine (2010) is one of my favorite movies. The sequel is a flaming pile of crap. Seemed like a script wasn't used at all. Scenes were too long and awkward.
3. The Matrix Sequels (2003) – Reloaded and Revolutions. Holy cow these were disappointing. The original is so great and these just really missed the mark. Part of it may have been all the hype surrounding the sequels. Keanu really makes some "out there" movies right?
4. The Hangover Part II (2011) – An utter abomination. I wish they had only made the first one. Just a really terrible movie experience all around. The third one wasn't great either but at least better than this one.
5. Caddyshack II (1988) – This makes the list because I remember seeing this as a 10 year old and being embarrassed by how bad it was. Substituting Bill Murray for Dan Aykroyd...ouch

Worst Sequels (L)

1. Star Wars: Episode 1 The Phantom Menace (1999) - Looking back...How unbelievably bad was this? How did George Lucas come up with this after 20 years of hypothetical day dreaming on bringing the franchise back. I don't even hate Jar-Jar and this one sucks.

2. Batman Returns (1992) - There could be multiple Batmans on this list but I will go with episode two. The Penguin was such a huge letdown from Nicholson's Joker. It just didn't click at all and fell flat.

3. Indiana Jones: Kingdom of the Crystal Skull (2008) - Shia is a questionable character but I can't even honestly say that was the reason. Some things are better left undisturbed. Not often does an iconic franchise take decades off and come back with a vengeance. Unless of course you are Star Wars.

4. Home Alone 3 (1997) - I kid you not...they tried to make a Home Alone movie without Macaualy Culken.

5. Ocean's 12 (2004) - This just has no excuse honestly. I realize the original set high expectations but what a bummer to see this cast stumble in a disappointing story.

Best 3rd Movie of a Trilogy (C)

1. Lord of the Rings: Return of the King (2005) – Best of the Lord of the Rings movies in my book. The scenes with Sam and Frodo are a little much but everything else was absolutely perfect. I would gladly bend the knee to Viggo Mortensen.

2. Indiana Jones and the Last Crusade (1989) – I know I've listed this one a few times already but there is no denying the staying power of this film. This was the perfect adventure film to an impressionable young mind.

3. Die Hard with a Vengeance (1995) - What a great installment to the Die Hard franchise. Way better than the second and right on par with the first. This is around the time I started taking notice of Samuel L. Jackson. I really wish the Die Hard series had ended here. "No he said Hey...Zeus."

4. Harry Potter and the Prisoner of Azkaban (2004) – The best Harry Potter film came with the third installment. I love time travel and Sirius Black. I wish there was more of Mr. Black in the subsequent films. There was definitely more info on him in the books.

5. Return of the Jedi (1983) – I love the opening to Jedi. The rescue mission at Jaba the Hut's place is the best. Those damn Ewoks almost ruined the movie though. I admit I enjoyed them as a kid but now I loathe them. Still a great third addition to the Star Wars franchise.

Best 3rd Movie of a Trilogy (L)

1. The Bourne Ultimatum (2007) - I love the Bourne movies and the third was the best by far. I could watch Jason Bourne stealthily sneak into Noah Vohsen's office all day long. They also tied it up to where we could have lived if that was the last one ever made.

2. Return of the Jedi (1983) - For 20 years this was a great bookend to an unbelievable trilogy that changed the game forever. Darth Vader's unmasking might be the biggest reveal in history and this really ended things on a satisfactory and emotional level.

3. Austin Powers: The Spy Who Shagged me (1999) - I was working at the theater at this time and I believe got Casey and I into a private midnight showing. This one was so ridiculous yet I can without a doubt say, I laughed more than the first two. Beyonce was probably my least favorite of the three leading ladies but everyone else was on point.

4. Indiana Jones and the Last Crusade (1989) - Adding Sean Connery into the mix is like adding the perfect amount of butter and salt to popcorn, it can make all the difference. All of the first three Indy movies were good which doesn't happen a lot.

5. Lord of the Rings: Return of the King (2003) - A fitting end to an epic trilogy. I will say however that this would have been higher if the ending of the movie didn't take an approximate 4 hours to wrap up. I can't remember all of the false finishes. Still.....adequate ending that did a good service to the series.

5. Holidays

For many, there are those must see movies around the holidays. If you don't belong to the many...fear not, Casey and Luke have complied some lists to watch during Christmas, Halloween, 4th of July and a few others. Merry Christmas ya filthy animals.

(C) = Casey
(L) = Luke

Christmas Movies (C)

1. Christmas Vacation (1989) – This is an absolute no brainer. This film is a part of the magic of Christmas to me. I can remember watching this at home when I was younger, at my grandparents' house, at college and now at my home. It's the perfect film. I'd even list it as my favorite in the Vacation franchise. If you go to an ugly sweater/Xmas costume party, just dress as Cousin Eddie and you will win.

2. Home Alone (1990) – This came out when I was eight years old. Had I seen this for the first time as an adult not sure it would have impacted me as much. But man this movie was the best. I feel like it's every kid's fantasy to be alone in the house and to be able to do whatever you want. That's when reality sets in and you realize what a little spoiled punk you are. I unsuccessfully tried to build traps in my house for hours. It's special to me now even more because I just watched it with my kids for the first time last Christmas. "Keep the change ya filthy animal."

3. Gremlins (1984) – Um...yes this is a Christmas movie. There's gremlins flying out of Christmas trees and stories of a Santa breaking his neck coming down the chimney. Gizmo is such a cute little guy and the Gremlins are so vile...but hilarious. Have you been hearing about all this alternate reality stuff where Stripe's name was Spike. Idiots. My son has been begging to see this...I know he won't be able to handle it...but I might show him anyway.

4. Elf (2003) – Great modern X-mas flick. This was also in the prime of Will Ferrell where he could do no wrong. This is a good one the whole family can watch. Also weird seeing Zooey Deschanel as a blonde.

5. It's a Wonderful Life (1946) – I'm including this because I remember watching it a lot with my sister growing up. And I feel I have a pretty good Wonderful

Life Jimmy Stewart impression. "Did ya hear that Clarence?"

Christmas Movies (L)
1. Home Alone (1990) - This movie was a freaking monster in the early 90's. I introduced Kale to it last year. I love it just as much as a thirty five year old as I did when I was eight. Even seeing a grown strung out Macaualy Culken can't ruin this for me.
2. It's a Wonderful Life (1946) - We are spoiled today and admittedly it is weird to watch a movie in black and white but from about 1988 to 1998 I would watch this movie every Christmas with my dad. So many life lessons here that ring true.
3. Christmas Vacation (1989) -The funniest Christmas movie of all time. A perfect time capsule. Chevy Chase's defining role in my opinion.
4. Elf (2003) - This has essentially become the Christmas Vacation for the generation younger than me. I dare you to turn on the TV any night during December and find this movie NOT on TV. Impossible I say.
5. Home Alone 2 (1992) - Not as good as the original but still very enjoyable. One of the first movies that I remember WAITING for to hit the theaters. I could barely wait. The world would look a lot different if Hillary Clinton helped Kevin McCallister with directions in this movie...

Halloween Movies (C)

1. Halloween III Season of the Witch (1982) – I love that every October 31st the Halloween franchise movies play for at least 24 hours. When I was younger I would always catch bits and pieces of Season of the Witch. However one year I finally found the time to take all of this one in and I was pleased. This is now my favorite of the series even without Michael Meyers. I would argue that Conal Cochran is way more evil than Meyers. This dude wants to kill every kid in the world. Also the Silver Shamrock jingle is phenomenal. If you don't like this movie I will fight you.

2. Trick R Treat (2007) – This was a more recent discovery. But I feel like if more people knew about this movie they would also love it. It's a Halloween flick that's told in different point of view stories that all come merging together at the end. I love the Trick or Treating rules this movie presents. This film also features the cutest little horror creature on film.

3. Halloween (1978) – Could probably be #2 but how lame is going back to back Halloween movies? This movie is the iconic Halloween classic that will last forever. Side note: At a Halloween college party, a friend of mine brought his friend who was dressed as Michael Meyers. This dude stayed in character ALL night long, he stood in a corner and just creepily stared at passersby.

4. Hocus Pocus (1993) – I watch this every Halloween and I still love it. I was 10 when this came out and I feel it's the perfect Halloween movie for a soft, sheltered 10 year old. I vividly remember ditching friends one year so I could be home in time to watch this classic. I also love that the dad is one of the bad guys from Dumb and Dumber (1994).

5. The Rocky Horror Picture Show (1975) – Another flick that is always shown on Halloween. I caught this for the first time at a friend's house and instantly fell in

love with the music. As of I've grown older it saddens me a bit that Rocky Horror has worked its way out of my rotation.

Halloween Movies (L)

1. Scream (1996) - Sure there are scarier movies but this came out at a time in my life where going to movies was all the rage. I was 13 and you bet I was there with a group that included females. Pretending not to be scared was my main strategy and I eagerly anticipated every move hoping not to jump and look cowardly.

2. The Ring (2002) - This move came out right around Halloween 2002. Not only was this movie freaky as crap, it was also the first movie I ever saw in the theaters with my wife. I never went back and watched it again but who can forget that little girl...

3. Halloween (1978) - I mean come on. Halloween not mentioned in the category named "Halloween" would be a travesty. The others were good for the most part (except Halloween 3, which would be tops on my worst Halloween movies) but the nostalgia of the original is where it is at.

4. I Know What You Did Last Summer (1997) - See #1 Scream except this time I was a year older (1997 vs Scream's 1996 release) and even more immature in not wanting to seem scared in front of females. Also, I was 14 and Jennifer Love Hewitt was in this so...

5. Poltergeist (1982) - I watched this one Saturday afternoon at home. It wasn't even Halloween and it was in broad daylight. It still scared the crap out of me and I can never see "TV fuzz" the same way again...

Movies to Watch on 4th of July (C)
1. Jaws (1975) – Nothing says 4th of July like a great white shark terrorizing the folks of Amity Island. Some people like to celebrate with cookouts, fireworks, etc. Me? I celebrate with Jaws. Why you ask? Because Jaws takes place during the 4th of July dummy!
2. Top Gun (1986) – When I think of America in the 80's I think of 3 things. 1) Tom Cruise 2) Fighter Jets 3) The Righteous Brothers. Seriously what a soundtrack! "I feel the need, the need for speed."
3. Independence Day (1996) – No brainer here. Gotta watch Independence Day on Independence Day. Rumor has it this is based on a true story. The truth is out there.
4. Die Hard (1988) – I know this is more of a Christmas movie but when I think of the John McClane he embodies the hard working American, who may or may not be having marital issues. Die Hard with a Vengeance (1995) also gives that feeling.
5. Coming to America (1988) – This story presents a couple of young men coming to America in search of the American Dream. How appropriate. "His mama call him Clay, I'mma call him Clay!" Remember when Arsenio Hall had a talk show?

Movies to Watch on 4th of July (L)

1. Independence Day (1996) - Duhhhhhhh! Will Smith, Jeff Goldblum, Aliens, fighting for our lives on July 4th. The only thing missing is a really good cookout scene.

2. 1776 (1972) - This list so far is easy. I mean come on now, our forefathers singing us through the constitution! Brilliant.

3. Lincoln (2012) - The best Lincoln biopic out there. Granted it only covered a sliver of his impact but what better way to celebrate the 4th by watching a movie about the President who helped maintain the celebration.

4. Saving Private Ryan (1998) -Veterans Day and July 4th are all about War for me. Maybe that's the guy in me but it is what I think about. I think this movie captures the sacrifice and horror of World War 2 as well any other.

5. Flags of our Fathers (2006) - See above. I really appreciate the specifics of this movie. Honing in on an iconic patriotic moment. Not an all-star cast by any means but Eastwood did great work here. Barry Pepper was in it (Hi Katie!) Sorry for the inside joke one reader will get.

Other Holiday Movies (C) Bonus

1. Trading Places (1983) – This a New Year classic. Not only is it a great all-around flick starring Eddie Murphy and Dan Aykroyd but it features a wonderful New Year's Eve party...on a train. As always Eddie steals the show. Also I have a friend in the frozen concentrated orange juice market. "Merry New Year!"

2. The Boondock Saints (1999) – A must watch on St. Patrick's Day...two Irish Twins seemingly turn into professional assassins overnight and take out a bunch of bad guys. Yea I know the actual St. Patrick would not approve. None the less, it's a fun movie to watch with a stand out performance from Willem Dafoe and we even get an early look at Darryl from The Walking Dead. Fun Fact: St. Patrick was not from Ireland.

3. Planes, Trains and Automobiles (1987) – This is the one and only movie you need to watch on Thanksgiving. This is one of those movies that I didn't fully understand when I first watched, but as I got older the sadder the film became. Poor Del. Steve Martin's character was very unlikeable by the way.

4. Mrs. Doubtfire (1993) – Not really a holiday per say, but I choose this movie for Father's/Mother's Day...wink. Always an entertaining film but I feel like I didn't start appreciating this film until later in life. It's so sad to watch this movie now and know that Robin is gone. "It was a run-by fruiting."

5. Groundhog Day (1993) – This is a rare case where the movie is better than the actual "holiday". Does anyone actually care about Groundhog Day? Besides a random town in Pennsylvania. At least there is a Bill Murray movie with the same name to make amends. Also to be noted I never actually watch this on Groundhog Day but c'mon it had to make the list. Fun fact: I watched this movie for the first time on laser disc.

6. Everything Else

This is arguably our most fun and most eclectic section. There's a little bit of everything for everybody...we have the Top 5 Movies Everyone Loves But Actually Suck...we have the Most Overrated Oscar Winners...we have our Favorite Fictional Movie Presidents...and the hits just keep on coming. You definitely don't want to miss this one.

(C) = Casey
(L) = Luke

Overrated Oscar Winners (C)

1. Chicago (2002) – Let me first start by saying I was entertained by this flick. But how on earth did this win best picture? Kind of felt like a poor man's Moulin Rouge. Lord of the Rings: Two Towers was robbed!

2. Unforgiven (1992) – Full disclosure I'm a John Wayne western fan. Having said that, this movie is soooo boring and I had zero enjoyment watching this. Eastwood shows zero range...and A Few Good Men was out there...they got it wrong.

3. Birdman (2014) – I think this film was too hyped up because I came in with high expectations. I really like Keaton and I really wanted to like this movie. But it was over my head I guess. I would have voted for American Sniper.

4. Slumdog Millionaire (2008) – Another film I enjoyed but I don't think it was Oscar worthy. It definitely wasn't better than The Curious Case of Benjamin Button. I blame Regis Philbin for this one.

5. Titanic (1997) – I haven't even seen this movie and I can tell you this may be the most overrated Oscar winner of all time. I have seen bits and pieces and it's all so cringe-worthy. "I'm the king of the world." Puke. L.A.Confidential should have won.

Overrated Oscar Winners (L)

1. The Kings Speech (2010) - I watched this on a plane ride to Ireland. That was the highlight for me. Yes there were some really good performances but do you want to know what this movie was about? A speech, soooooooooo yeah it was boring.
2. American Beauty (1999) - There were some really good performances in this but I remember just being really sad while watching this. Adultery, lust, murder, greed amongst others didn't give me the warm and fuzzies. It didn't wow me and there are some tough choices to be made in this category.
3. Platoon (1986) - Apparently you must be depressing to get an Oscar nomination. When I finished Platoon, I felt like I needed to eat a gallon of ice cream and buy a kitten to get my life back on track.
4. The Sting (1973) - I hate putting this here but this won an Oscar? I liked it, don't get me wrong but it didn't give me the "Oscar Feeling".
5. Shakespeare in Love (1998) - This honestly finds its way onto the list for one reason. I know I have seen it but I can't tell you a single thing about it. If it didn't grab my attention enough to remember a single thing 20 years later, then it is on this list.

Movies that Everyone Loves but Actually Suck (C)

1. Fight Club (1999) – This is going to be unpopular but I don't get the love for this movie. I don't find it to be clever at all. The movie has a decent twist at the end but does that make it a great movie? Nope. Also to be noted I found Edward Norton to be obnoxious. I wish people took a cue from this movie and never actually talked about Fight Club.

2. Rudy (1993) – The movie is about as accurate as Bay's Pearl Harbor (2001) flick. This was a popular movie to watch before high school football games. I wasn't inspired one bit. Maybe that's why our team sucked.

3. A Clockwork Orange (1971) – Sorry but this movie sucks. I was totally fine with this guy being mistreated after what he does in the beginning of the film. Maybe that's the statement of the film, but it's so dumb and boring. Frankly I'd rather be watching Project Runway.

4. Batman Begins (2005) – Is Christian Bale the worst batman? Well no, since Affleck put on the suit. Is this the worst Batman movie? Probably. Is Bale's Batman voice terrible? No doubt. The only positive is that it paved the way for the Dark Knight.

5. Lethal Weapon (1987) – I watched this film for the first time in 2017 so that's probably part of the problem. I also had my buddy Sean hyping this movie up to me. So then I watched it...and I found it to be super lame. I guess I always thought these movies were supposed to be funny. So maybe I had some unfair expectations. Then I watched Lethal Weapon 2 (1989) and really enjoyed it. In Summation I only like Lethal Weapon 2.

Movies that Everyone Loves but Actually Suck (L)

1. The Matrix (1999) - Literally all of my closest friends raved about this and essentially forced me to watch it. My reaction was somewhere between "That's it?" and "What the heck?" Also, any movie with Keanu Reaves can't be that good.

2. The Big Lebowski (1998) - I quite honestly have no idea how this is a cult classic. It gets all kinds of love but for me, it is simply the 39th best movie of 1998.

3. Raging Bull (1980) - This is one that gets loads of unwarranted praise. I watched this in the Ozarks... thinking LeMotta is a huge turd is all I remember. De Niro was good, I get it but he usually is, so why should this stand out?

4. Half Baked (1998) - Are we going to be doing a "Top 5 most annoying movies of all time"? Some of my friends in high school got into weed and it became all they talked about. It annoyed the heck out of me. Guess what their favorite movie was that they wanted to watch ALL the time? You guessed it and that too annoyed the heck out of me.

5. Saw (2004) - I like scary movies but I like thought put into them. I feel like Saw was based on one question and one question alone..."What is the grossest way possible to kill someone?"

Movies I Saw at Too Young of an Age (C)

1. The Thing (1982) – I would guess I was five or six. My family and I were staying in a hotel and we were watching a family friendly movie on HBO. Long story short...my mom, dad and sister all fell asleep...and The Thing came on after the family friendly movie. I didn't even know what I was getting into until the dog kennel scene. It was the most terrifying moment of my early life. I was never able to shake this movie from my memory. I can't put my finger on the exact date but as I got older I kept watching it...like over and over. As of 2018 it's my favorite movie of all time.

2. Jaws (1975) – I was at least in elementary school when I first watched Jaws. I'll guess I was in first grade. This is one of my dad's favorite films so naturally I watched this with him, not sure if it was intentional or not. To his credit, I do remember him warning me about stuff about to happen, but after seeing those lifeless shark eyes I was terrified of open water. I was even a little unsure about swimming pools. Much like The Thing this is now one of my all-time favorite films.

3. A Nightmare on Elm Street (1984) – Freddy freaking Krueger. Man that guy was absolutely frightening. I watched this during Halloween in my youth. Bad decision. A creepy killer who haunts you in your dreams? Well that's a guaranteed nightmare for a little kid. I don't really like these films in my adulthood. I think Dream Warriors is cool but the others I'm pretty indifferent to.

4. Killer Clowns from Outer Space (1988) – If clowns weren't scary enough add in the element of killer alien clowns. I remember seeing this at the local video store back in the day and wanting nothing to do with it. Then I stumbled across it at a family member's house and I just couldn't stop watching. This movie is pretty awful and I haven't watched it in conservatively about 20 years.

5. Empire of the Sun (1987) - I have no idea why we sat down as a family to watch this. I was young when I first saw this and I vividly remember the hardships facing young Christian Bale. The scene where he is separated from his mother tore my heart out. The main theme song is absolutely beautiful. I believe I had it on a mixed CD from college.

Movies I Saw at Too Young of an Age (L)
1. Boyz in the Hood (1991) - I can't really remember anything about this movie other than I saw it at an embarrassingly young age. My friend at the time made us watch it one day at his house. I lost touch with this friend in junior high but my old friend coincidentally has been in prison many times.
2. Howard the Duck (1986) - My mom went through a phase where she really liked ducks. I thought it would be a great idea to rent the movie Howard the Duck when I was a wee little boy. Mom clearly did not read the back of the VHS box.
3. Problem Child 2 (1991) - I was embarrassed to see this in the theaters. It was a very immature movie. I realized that as an eight year old mind you.
4. Posse (1993) - My babysitter rented this movie when I was 10. I was pushing for Three Ninjas (1992) but instead he thought it would be a great idea for me to watch this rated R movie about cowboys in the wild west. I wanted to be cool so I had to "no sell" being scared and uncomfortable the entire time.
5. Under Siege (1992) - I was around 11 when I saw this movie. I remember borrowing this from an uncle or cousin. I can't quite remember which. What I can remember is that there was a naked lady in the movie. Most likely the first time I saw this in a film. I couldn't decide if I should tell somebody, or just rewind it and watch it again.

Movies that Were Great as Kids But Now Suck (C)

1. Howard the Duck (1986) – A funny little duck man walking around Earth cracking wise…what's not to love? I really thought I loved this movie until I watched it again recently. I enjoyed Lea Thompson in this but that's about it. This is also a pretty messed up movie…a lot of adult things I missed as a kid.

2. Harry and the Hendersons (1987) – A frequently rented film at the Heaton house. This is one I wish I hadn't gone back and watched recently. It was beyond boring, I could barely make it through the whole film, which blows my mind because I remember loving it as a kid. I guess having a Sasquatch in the movie really made it for me. John Lithgow is so unlikeable in this role as well.

3. No Holds Barred (1989) – This is an example of a movie I still really enjoy BUT…I thought it was a big deal in my youth. Like this was one of the greatest films ever made. It had my guy, Hulk Hogan, featured in a "big budget" film that came to movie theaters and everything. It was much later in life that I realized what a joke this movie was. To reiterate, I do still like this movie. Kurt Fuller was an amazing villain as well.

4. Blank Check (1994) – I remember renting Blank Check from Prestige Video numerous times. I was so in love with this film. I wanted to be Preston so bad. He had a cool house, cool toys, a cool computer and literally anything else he wanted. So many great memories. Then I watched it again as an adult. 1) Its embarrassing to watch 2) this movie sends a terrible message to kids. I think I held this in high regard because the main character was Andy on Family Ties, which everyone knows is the best TV show of all time.

5. Pee-wee's Big Adventure (1985) – This could be controversial. Let me again start by saying I do still

enjoy watching Pee-wee when I'm in a certain mood. When I was younger this too seemed like a larger than life flick. It seemed there were real consequences and a lot at stake for Pee-wee. I really wanted him to find that bike. I just showed this to my older kids not long ago and while I enjoyed it...the magic is gone.

Movies that Were Great as Kids But Now Suck (L)

1. Earnest Goes to Camp (1987) - I share the same last name as Earnest P but I can't vouch for him any longer. I remember finding this hilarious and now I find it embarrassing that I was a huge fan of this series. However I do still get behind the idea of snapping turtles being launched with parachutes.

2. The Mask (1994) - Honestly anything from Jim Carey not named Dumb and Dumber (1994) or The Truman Show (1998) sucks. I hate to say it because the guy was on fire and I loved the Mask when it came out. I watched a few minutes of the movie a couple years ago and needed therapy because of the guilt associated with thinking it was good as a kid.

3. Super Mario Brothers (1993) - I don't even really know what to say here....I liked it. I am now remorseful for that choice.

4. The Mighty Ducks (1992) - I really feel bad about this, truly I do. But have any of you watched this recently. If not, just get a block of cheese from your local grocery store and stare at it for 90 minutes. I do however still reference the triple deke anytime I catch a hockey game.

5. Police Academy (1984) - I rented the crap out of this whole series around 1990. That said, I have to face the facts after watching them in recent years....they are barely funny.

Popular Movies I Haven't Seen (C)

1. Titanic (1997) – It makes me sick that people love this movie so much. I've never seen it and don't plan on ever watching it. In '97 I saw soooo many movies in theaters and didn't see this one on purpose. I can't really pinpoint the reason why, but I hate this movie.

2. Schindler's List (1995) – This is one I really should watch. It's beloved by everyone I've talked to. This one just slipped through the cracks. I'm adding it to my Netflix DVD queue now.

3. Sleepless in Seattle (1993) – I was only 11 when this came out, so naturally I wasn't into the romantic comedy. I do like Tom and Meg…ya know I may throw this on the queue as well. Probably not though.

4. Casablanca (1942) – I know all the quotes from this movie…just haven't actually seen it. It's already on my Netflix queue, however it keeps getting bumped down further and further. I just looked and it is currently sitting at #28 in the queue.

5. Good Will Hunting (1997) – Just never had any interest in seeing this. I love Robin, I really like Matt Damon, and I kind of like Affleck (I don't like Affleck) so it seems I should have seen this at some point. At this point in time I have no plans to see it.

Popular Movies I Haven't Seen (L)

1. The Godfather (1972) - Not only have I not seen the Godfather, I haven't seen ANY of the Godfathers. At this point in my life, I barely have time to tie my shoes, so I don't foresee myself taking nine plus hours to watch this trilogy.

2. Jaws (1975) - I am quickly realizing that this list may completely discredit me from participating in this movie project. I have seen pieces but not once have I sat down to intentionally watch Jaws. I did however thoroughly enjoy the ride at Universal Studios.

3. Fight Club (1999) - Everyone and their pet raved about this movie in high school. It still has a massive cult following and I still have yet to watch it or find the motivation to want too.

4. Guardians of the Galaxy (2014) - I believe this movie set records at the box office recently. I also believe I don't give two craps about ever seeing this movie. Sorry Dave Bautista.

5. Schindler's List (1993) - I honestly am more embarrassed about this one than any other. The topic of this film is obviously very sensitive and I have trouble watching anything to do with it.

Movies I Watched in School (C)

1. The Patriot (2000) – Watched this one for the first time in a high school history class. I remember running out to the store to buy it that same week. Mel Gibson was on top of the world and Heath Ledger was a rising star...oh how times have changed. Also I'm sure it was somewhat common of the time period but I was a little uncomfortable with Mel hooking up with his dead wife's sister at the end.

2. Can't Buy Me Love (1987) – I was in eighth grade and the school year was coming to an end. We had a super cool Spanish teacher that showed us this movie for no reason other than she loved it. The world needs more teachers like that!

3. The Man Who Shot Liberty Valance (1962) – In high school I took an American History Through Film class, which is where I first saw this one. I grew up in a pro John Wayne household so it was kind of strange I hadn't already seen this. The film had a more serious tone than what I was accustomed to, but still a really good movie. Jimmy Stewart is pretty awesome in this as well.

4. Say Anything (1989) – I had another really cool teacher in my high school Interpersonal Communications class. Oddly enough Luke was in the class as well. A lot of hijinks went down but we'll save that for another book. Cusack with the boombox held high overhead screams 80's. To be noted we also watched Some Kind of Wonderful (1987) in this same class.

5. Enemy of the State (1998) – I don't want to sound like a hater, but remember when Will Smith was entertaining? The Fresh Prince of Bel-Air really set the tone for a great career that seemingly fizzled out in the late 2000's. Having said all that, I still love Will. He and Hackman are both solid in this flick.

Movies I Watched in School (L)

1. Last of the Mohicans (1992) - I watched this for the first time in history class in high school. A unique choice really but man something like this in school was legit.

2. The Crucible (1996) - Apparently Jacksonville High School really appreciates Daniel Day Lewis. I cakewalked through the book, but man, the movie really got me. I nearly cried in front of girls and that was unacceptable. "More weight..."

3. The Man Who Shot Liberty Valence (1962) - I took an American History Through Film class. Thank God I was an upperclassman because you know everyone in the school tried to get in this class. We literally watched movies and talked about them. Looking back, this class was terrible. The choices weren't even that historically applicable but hey....score for us kids!

4. Sands of Iwo Jima (1949) - Another classic war movie thanks to that cakewalk class in high school! Seriously...we watched John Wayne movies and wrote craptastic papers on them. I had never really experienced a non-western John Wayne movie. Really solid movie for this or any time period.

5. Lost in Translation (2003) - True story. I took a personal communications class in college. For a time, our teacher just showed us emotionally driven movies. When asked why, she admitted it was a rough time in her marriage. Very sad story but memorable. Bill Murray was money and a young Scarlet Johannsen made a name for herself. I also am still searching for that Asian Techno song played in the party montage.

Movies I've Recently Rented (C)

1. The Big Sick (2017) - I threw this on the DVD queue for my wife. We watched it recently and I'll be damned, it was a good movie. Kumail Nanjiani is freakin' hilarious for starters then you factor in a very non-conventional love story. It was great to see Ray Romano doing something other than a wooly mammoth voice as well.

2. Night of the Creeps (1986) – I just watched this for the first time about a month ago. I kept hearing about how great this was and just never got around to watching it. I think it was a little hyped but I did enjoy the film. Tom Atkins rules.

3. Get Out (2017) – Another recent rental, this was a weird movie. It was unlike anything I had seen before. Very creepy feel with some great twists. Pretty enjoyable flick.

4. Life (2017) – This movie is basically The Thing (1982) but set in space. Solid cast and some surprising early deaths.

5. Spider-Man: Homecoming (2017) – I will say this may be the best Spider-Man movie ever made...but also know that I loathe those Toby Maguire flicks. Bonus points for getting Michael Keaton on board. Entertaining film overall.

Movies I've Recently Rented (L)

1. Bridge of Spies (2015) - Allison and I have been playing catch up on movies for the last two and half years. Weird...our youngest son is two and a half. Anyway, we recently watched this Spielberg film. As expected, you can't go wrong with Spielberg and Hanks as a combo. I was also pleasantly surprised to research post-movie and discover that they tried hard to maintain historical accuracy.

2. The House (2017) - I watched this on a plane recently. What is it about Will Ferrell screaming? He could scream about anything and I would laugh hysterically. Amy Pohler is also a favorite of mine so I really dug this goofy comedy.

3. The Martian (2015) - What a freaking cast! Matt Damon is good and I dug the story. Small bit pieces by Kristen Wiig and Donald Glover added to my enjoyment. Two thumbs up.

4. Ghostbusters (2016) - I really like the ladies involved but it fell kind of flat for me. Part of it could have been that the DVD froze and we had to finish it at a later date. Wiig is a personal favorite of mine from her dominance on SNL. Not bad but not great either.

5. Jack Ryan: Shadow Recruit (2014) - We are big fans of this genre. This one was good but it was missing something. I can't quite put my finger on it. Costner was a nice little addition and I don't have anything against Pine. He was solid. I think I held this movie in unrealistic comparisons to its predecessors.

Performances by a Musician (C)

1. David Bowie in the Labyrinth (1986) – This movie will forever remind me of my sister. She even had that killer soundtrack on CD, which we listened to a lot. David Bowie was larger than life in this movie. There was something so scary yet appealing about his character...and no it wasn't the tights. The Goblin King is such a fantastic role. And Bowie singing "Dance Magic Dance" always brings a smile to my face. Jennifer Connelly was a tad bit annoying. "You remind of the Babe."

2. Madonna in A League of Their Own (1992) – Say what you will about Madonna but there is no denying her awesomeness as "All the way Mae". Almost chose her performance as Breathless Mahoney in Dick Tracy (1990), but Mae is better.

3. Alice Cooper in Wayne's World (1992) – "Actually, it's pronounced "mill-e-wah-que" which is Algonquin for the good land." Cooper is only in this movie for a few minutes but the performance is legendary. Had he been featured in the movie more I might have listed him higher. Another great cameo in Prince of Darkness (1987) where he impales a guy with a bike.

4. Ice Cube in Friday (1995) – Ice Cube has a list of entertaining roles but "Craig" is his best. The plotline is pretty absurd but it's still entertaining. This film also put Chris Tucker on the map, but this isn't about Smokey, this is about Craig. It's very rewarding to see him knock out Deebo. "Bye Felicia."

5. Huey Lewis in Back to the Future (1985) – This is just a cameo but it's the perfect cameo. He plays the uptight talent judge who tells Marty McFly, "I'm afraid you're just too darn loud." Classic.

Performance by a Musician (L)

1. David Bowie in Labyrinth (1986) - I sang " Dance Magic Dance", just last week in the car. No kidding. I was obsessed with this movie as a kid. Only when I grew up did I learn that the weird guy was an acclaimed musician. I can't think of anyone else who could have pulled that role off.

2. Madonna in A League of Their Own (1992) - Not a big fan of Madonna but she was awesome in her role. Also, gun to my head before watching and I would have pegged her as a center fielder.

3. Alice Cooper in Wayne's World (1992) - 75% of my knowledge about Milwaukee comes from Alice in this movie. He hit a home run here. Perfect amount of time for a scene stealer. I remember after watching the movie, Dad told me about some of his real life concert antics. I was stunned.

4. Snoop Dogg in Old School (2003) - I don't know why but I always remember being shocked that he showed up at their house party. I'm guessing that Snoop Dogg sucks as an actor, which is why I appreciate them just making him stick to music.

5. Alanis Morrisette in Dogma (1999) - She didn't do anything special, and in fact I'm not sure she even spoke. This is another one of those cameos that I just always remember. The artist who gave us Jagged Little Pill being portrayed as God was crazy.

Fictional Movie Presidents (C)

1. Harrison Ford as James Marshal in Air Force One (1997) – This was a no brainer as my #1. It took a little more research for #2-5 but the top spot is reserved for presidents that throw terrorists off of planes. "Get off my plane."

2. Bill Pullman as Thomas J. Whitmore in Independence Day (1996) – Pullman is pretty cool, as president he hops in a jet to defend the Earth from alien invaders. He also gives a pretty motivating speech. I'd vote for him.

3. Donald Pleasence as "The President" In Escape from New York (1981) – I was torn on this one. Pleasence is kind of a turd of a president, I don't think he actually cares about the people who died to save his butt…HOWEVER he does mow down the Duke with a machine gun and totally saves Snake Plissken's hide. So for that I salute you Donald Pleasence. Also weird that a Brit is the American president.

4. Jamie Foxx as James Sawyer in White House Down (2013) – James Sawyer has to be the coolest fake president. For instance he has a collection of Jordans…that's incredible. Kind of strange that this came out the same time as Olympus has Fallen (2013)…they are basically the same movie, except Jamie Foxx is way better than Aaron Eckhart.

5. Charlie Sheen as President Rathcock in Machete Kills (2013) – Sheen has to make the list because he is basically just playing the role as himself. Also weird that Charlie's dad was also a great fictional president on "The West Wing".

Fictional Movie Presidents (L)

1. Bill Pullman as Thomas J. Whitmore in Independence Day (1996) - It took me half of a second to list Bill #1 here. Dude physically fought aliens himself moments after losing his wife. When I first heard his speech before the final fight, I almost signed up for the Air Force.

2. Harrison Ford as James Marshal in Air Force One (1997) - It was a simpler time. Presidents beat the snot out of terrorists instead of baiting them on Twitter. Ahhhh the 1990's. Harrison really can't do much wrong, except for that last Indiana Jones movie, but I digress...

3. Michael Douglas as Andrew Shepherd in The American President (1995) - Douglas nailed it in this romantic comedy. What a novel idea, a bachelor president. I really liked this change of pace portrayal of a president in film.

4. Tim Robbins as "The President" in Austin Powers: The Spy Who Shagged Me (1999) - It wasn't long but it was funny. Not only is it good to see a president portrayed in a ridiculous comedy, but I thought it was another feather in Tim Robbin's cap. The guy can find a role in any type of movie. Super underrated.

5. Bruce Greenwood as "The President" in National Treasure: Book of Secrets (2007) - Not gonna lie. I would be hard pressed to tell you anything about Mr. Greenwood. In fact, I had to look up his name. I just remember thinking that the guy looked so "presidential" and was smooth. Greenwood in 2020.

Movie Villains (C)
1. Darth Vader from Star Wars (1977) – Whether you like Star Wars or not, Darth Vader has to be the most recognizable villain ever! From his helmet, breathing apparatus and James Earl Jones voice… he is a legit bad ass. Oh and he can force choke people. Seriously the worst thing the Star Wars franchise ever did was introduce the Emperor as Darth's superior. Darth Vader answers to no one!
2. The Joker from Batman (1989) – "Ever dance with the Devil in the pale moonlight?" Jack Nicholson is the Joker in my mind. This was such a fantastic performance. The Joker was funny but also a terrifying psycho.
3. The Terminators from Terminator (1984) and Terminator 2 (1991) – The original Arnold Terminator was such a beast. He was a relentless killing machine with some cool living tissue scenes (including an eyeball). The T-1000 was literally an upgraded killing machine. He felt even more unstoppable than Arnold which is what really made T2 so great. So I lump these two villains together because they are both deserving of the #3 spot.
4. Alex Forrest from Fatal Attraction (1987) – Going less mainstream here…but is there anything more frightening than a crazy ex-girlfriend? Like I'd rather take on an axe murder. One moment everything is normal and then all of the sudden the pet bunny is boiling in a pot of water on the stove.
5. Hannibal Lecter from The Silence of the Lambs (1991) – Dr. Lecter has to make the list. Such an interesting villain. An educated cannibal? That's right. Who happens to be versed in profiling serial killers as well…such talents. The straight jacket/face guard is an image I will never shake.

Movie Villains (L)

1. Anton Chigurh from No Country for Old Men (2007) - I can't think of a movie where I was more restless every time the villain was on screen. Javier scared the crap out of me. My whole body tensed up from the moment that character appeared.

2. Palpatine/Emperor from The Star Wars Franchise - Tempting to put Darth Vader here but there are redemptive qualities to Darth. Palpatine was the one who destroyed the special Anikan Skywalker by mind games and the dark side of the force. As bad as the prequels were, it made The Emperor even worse. Slowly seeing him seize power and manipulate Anikan was incredibly agonizing.

3. Hannibal Lector from Silence of the Lambs (1991) - A testament to Anthony Hopkins, Dr. Lector was terrifying yet somehow you kind of liked him. While he was somewhat likeable...at the end of the day he was eating people. This qualifies him as a "villain" to me.

4. Michael Meyers from Halloween (1978) - Of all the franchise slasher films, Meyers is the one that scared me the most. The others were pretty comic book like for me. The terrifying white mask with the musical underscore drove him home and into this list.

5. The Joker from the Dark Knight (2008) - Heath Ledger nailed it. I think people would say that even if he didn't die at a young age shortly after its release. Heck, you could even mention Jack Nicholson here. They both played this villain well.

Movie Crushes (C)

1. Elisabeth Shue – My first movie crush was her in Adventures in Babysitting (1987). I was praying she would be my next babysitter…didn't happen. "Don't nobody leave here without singing the blues."

2. Salma Hayek – Any movie she is in, but if I had to pick only one I'd say Wild Wild West (1999).

3. Mia Sara – I was in love with Sloane Peterson from Ferris Bueller's Day Off (1986) for at least a few years.

4. Sandra Bullock – As already noted, I'm pro-Sandra Bullock. I had a big crush on her from her Demolition Man (1993) role.

5. Jennifer Lopez – I was and am a big J-Lo fan still to this day. She can do it all…sing, act and she is gorgeous. This is kind of weird but I loved her in Anaconda (1997). Although it was very unbelievable she was romantically linked to Eric Stoltz. He could never pull that off.

Movie Crushes (L)

1. Ariana Richards - You're probably asking yourself who this is. In what will be my most embarrassing entry, I will tell you exactly who she is. She is the girl in Jurassic Park who went on to do nothing else in Hollywood. Those teeny bop magazines were all the rage at Salem Lutheran School during this time. I had such a crush on this young lady that I had a female classmate send her fan mail on my behalf. I wish I was kidding. I can also report that 24 years later, she has yet to respond to me.

2. Natalie Portman - Not only is she an attractive woman, I think Portman is just so cool. In almost every movie she is in, you just feel like she would be the most fun person in the world to hang out with. Ok, maybe not Black Swan (2010), but you get my point.

3. Meg Ryan - I am going to go ahead and make a "not so nice" remark right here...Meg hasn't aged well. I am not sure if she has had too much work done or what, but I digress. In the mid to late 90's, Meg was breathtaking and always seemed to play those "take home to mom" type characters. A famous quote I once gave my friend Nick, "Give me Meg or give me death."

4. Rachel McAdams - A gorgeous lady in everything she is in. She was even a nasty cheating jezebel in Midnight in Paris (2011) and I didn't even care. I would say though that she was peak "crushable" in The Notebook (2004) or The Vow (2012).

5. Gwyneth Paltrow - There was a period in the late 90's where I really dug Gwyneth. I thought she was adorable in Shallow Hal (2001), Duets (2000) and Bounce (2000).

Worst Endings (C)

1. The Village (2004) – So obviously there will be major spoilers on this list. This in my mind was the downfall of M. Night Shyamalan. This movie had a good look and a creepy vibe. The monsters coming into the village were so interesting. Unfortunately at this point in M Knight's career you knew a twist was coming. I remember leaning over to Luke like 25 minutes into this film and saying "this better not be set in present day." Fast forward to the end and the movie is set in present day. The villagers had removed themselves and their families from the real world. Lame.

2. Batman V Superman: Dawn of Justice (2016) – I was kind of excited to see this movie. Even though Ben Affleck is hot garbage. The film wasn't bad, fairly entertaining even, but then came the Superman/Batman fight scene…I came really close to just stopping the movie. If you haven't already seen this movie let me save you some time. Superman is destroying Batman but then they discover their moms have the same name and the fight ends. Embarrassing.

3. Matrix Revolutions (2003) – So Neo, "the One", is killed. Then I think some of the machines are trying to bring him back to life but then everything resets? Yea I'm asking, I'm not even sure what I watched. Then it's just over. If I had a time machine the first thing I'd do is go back in time to stop the Matrix sequels from being made. Horrible.

4. The Happening (2008) – Another M Knight movie…and to be fair the entire movie is awful. I guess I can go with the plants releasing a toxin into the air attacking the human population. However, at the end the main characters decide they will go outside and live their last moments together and the toxins in the air have just disappeared…for no reason. Then only to have a twist in the final scene of yet another plant attack in Paris…makes no sense.

5. Star Wars Episode III: Revenge of the Sith (2005) – The final installment of a disappointing prequel trilogy.

Hayden Christensen was a lame Darth and the transformation at the end was such a letdown. The thing I hated most was all the Jedi being killed off...including a bunch of little Jedi kids. Darth can never be redeemed.

Worst Endings (L)

1. Arlington Road (1999) - I fully admit that it is unrealistic to have the "good guys" always win. A curveball is sometimes needed. I was not digging this curveball and the talent of Tim Robbins be darned. I was so disheartened after viewing this in the theater. Domestic terrorism is only sadder now in 2018.

2. War of the Worlds (2005) - An indestructible army of alien soldiers were defeated. Who was the hero? The knight in shining armor? It was the flu...the aliens got the flu.

3. Titanic (1997) - This is a good movie and many things can be said here. In fact, I really like it so why is it on this list? Rose has a 3-4 day love affair with Jack. Jack tragically dies (obviously room on the makeshift raft mind you). As the movie plays out, we find out that Rose went on, married a good man and has what appears to be a good family. So at the end when the symbolism comes of her passing on into the afterlife, she is welcomed into eternity by...Jack. What the heck happened to the solid guy she spent most of her life with? You know, the father of her children? That has always bothered me. This unnamed guy is an afterthought as she passes on.

4. The Game (1997) - Michael Douglas is good but I remember watching this on VHS when I was a teenager. Even then I was astonished that they would jeopardize lives for this "game." So stupid to think it could all be choreographed. Whoever organized this game should have been put in jail for negligence.

5. Indiana Jones: The Kingdom of the Crystal Skull (2008) - Indiana Jones is all about biblical archeology and mythology. There is enough craptastic alien encounter movies out there. Soiling this franchise with this was a fart in church for me.

Wasted Casts (C)

1. Ocean's Twelve (2004) – Clooney, Pitt, Damon, Roberts, Zeta-Jones, Casey Affleck, Scott Caan, Andy Garcia, Cheedle, Bernie Mac, Elliott Gould and Robbie Coltrane...are you kidding me? What a freakin' dog turd this movie was. Especially coming off the heels of the first film. This has to be the most wasted cast EVER!

2. Pearl Harbor (2001) – Ok to be fair this movie sucks mostly due to the unreal true story it tries to tell but then to waste the lesser Affleck, Josh Hartnett, Kate Beckinsale, Cuba Gooding Jr., Alec Baldwin, Jennifer Garner, Jon Voight, Michael Shannon, Dan Aykroyd and William Fichtner...heinous.

3. Batman Forever (1995) – I actually enjoy this film BUT this had potential to be the best Batman movie...which obviously didn't happen. Val Kilmer was criminally under-utilized in this movie. They should have given him more freedom to be Bruce Wayne. Jim Carrey is great in this film but Tommy Lee Jones could have done better. This film also had Nicole Kidman, Chris O'Donnell and Drew Barrymore. Should have been much better.

4. 3,000 Miles to Graceland (2001) – This movie hurts my heart. I wanted to love it, or at least like it. It features two of my favorites in the BIZ (Kurt Russell and Kevin Costner). Then you add in some nice work from Christian Slater, Courteney Cox, Kevin Pollak, Jon Lovitz, Thomas Haden Church and Ice-T. Let's be honest this movie is horrendous. I'm sorry Kurt!

5. Wolf of Wall Street (2013) – How do you make a bad movie with DiCaprio, McConaughey, Jonah Hill and Margot Robbie? See this movie for the answer. This film could have used much, much, much better editing. The scenes go on way too long and the jokes do not work. Like they are embarrassing to hear. I hated to see Jonah and Leo on screen drowning in terrible

dialogue. Also McConaughey is only in the movie for like two minutes...immediate red flag.

Wasted Casts (L)
1. Ocean's Twelve (2004) - This cast was loaded and the follow up to a great first installment was terrible in my opinion. I distinctly remember walking away disappointed. How could that be with this ensemble?
2. He's Just Not That Into You (2009) - I didn't expect to see the best movie of all time here but I mean...at least be a decent romantic comedy right? The stars in this movie are insane. How did they afford this cast? What secrets did the powers to be have on these guys and gals? Whatever it was, they did not make it count.
3. Alexander (2004) - On paper, this movie should have been wayyyy better than it was. I am not a huge Colin Farrell fan by any means but this cast, along with this story should have been approximately 14 times more engrossing.
4. Burn After Reading (2008) - I couldn't even make it to the end of the movie. Not sure if it was the uniqueness of a Coen Brothers movie but this was abysmal. There is no way a movie headlined by Pitt and Clooney should be this bad. The cast was filled out with very accomplished complimentary pieces as well. This found its way back into the Netflix sleeve quickly.
5. Gangster Squad (2013) - I will be honest, I Googled "Bad movies with a great cast" and this popped up. I know I have seen this movie....can't tell you a darn thing about it. The fact that a movie has Gosling, Penn, Brolin AND Emma Stone yet I can't remember it speaks volumes.

Movies I Randomly Recommend (C)

1. The Red Violin (1998) – I'm guessing most have not seen this movie. Great story that follows a red violin as it travels from owner to owner spanning over centuries. Well done movie that reminds me of one of Luke's favorite books…*The Girl in the Hyacinth Blue*. All joking aside the book and film are both really good!

2. Last of the Mohicans (1992) – This was my sister's favorite movie in the 90's and very well still could be her favorite film. I would say she has seen it conservatively 947 times, and of those 947 I think I watched with her for at least 10 of those. Having said that, this movie is pretty good, but what absolutely takes the cake…is the amazing score. It gets me jacked up to go running through waterfalls and fighting off enemies.

3. Road House (1989) – I can't believe this hasn't made a list yet. This is a great 80's flick and wonderful performance from Patrick Swayze. This is also probably the coolest Sam Elliot appearance as well. You gotta love a movie that centers around bouncers at a bar. I love how little police presence there is in the movie even though the bad guys are causing so much damage and even committing murder. Swayze has a killer throat rip. Wrestler alert…Terry Funk.

4. The Lost Boys (1987) – A movie that would probably never make a top five list but still a movie that needs to be seen. This film takes me back to a simpler time…a time when the Coreys were on top of the world…and when Kiefer Sutherland was a bad ass vampire. This is definitely a must see.

5. Ghosts of Mars (2001) – This is a must see if you're a John Carpenter fan. It was originally supposed to be a Snake Plissken movie but then they went a different direction. It's still pretty interesting when you watch the movie and think of it as a Snake Plissken movie, Ice Cube is even wearing the camo pants.

Movies I Randomly Recommend (L)

1. The Lookout (2007) - I really like Joseph Gordon-Levitt's work here and Jeff Daniels is always a welcomed addition. A thriller that flew under the radar for sure. There was a big plot hole towards the end. Go see this and we can discuss!
2. So I Married an Axe Murderer (1993) - I really like this old comedy. Before Mike Myers became Wayne and Austin. The subtle humor was good, the plot just ridiculous enough. Please also notice Central Illinois right next to Mike's head in the final scene. Easter Egg!
3. Albino Alligator (1996) - I need to see this again. If drilled on the exact premise, I would fail. What I can tell you is that I rented this like three times in 1999 and made my friends watch it. Really good cast and an interesting script.
4. Overboard (1987) - One of those 1980's classics that I ended up watching over and over on VHS because it was one of the random options available to me. Casey's boy Kurt Russell gives us the goods here.
5. Martha Marcy May Marlene (2011) - A raw and gritty indie flick. John Hawkes nails his role here and the non-Full House Olson sister proves she's the best of the bunch. You kind of leave the movie worried about how much of this really happens but I suppose that's the point.

Movies I Discovered Way Too Late (C) Bonus

1. Fast Times at Ridgemont High (1982) – Watched this for the first time in 2017! I know calm down everyone. I don't know what to say. It just slipped through the cracks. I never had the desire to see it. I knew of the Spicoli character and judged a book by its cover. I had no idea how amazing the movie was. The opening features an 80's mall scene which set the tone for a great experience. This movie had a little bit of a dark side to it as well which I was not expecting. "I hope you had a hell of a piss Arnold."

2. The Golden Child (1986) Saw this for the first time in probably 2014. This has to be one of Eddie's most underrated flicks. I don't ever remember this movie even being discussed in my circle of friends in the 80's and 90's. So glad I stumbled upon this on Netflix. "So you're just gonna let that booger freeze up on your jacket like that?"

3. Tango and Cash (1989) – I had always caught bits and pieces of this but never actually sat down to watch it all until a few years ago. Stallone and Curt are such a great duo. I'm mad at myself for waiting so long. "FUBAR, big time."

4. Sixteen Candles (1984) – Not sure how this slipped by, I've always been a big John Hughes fan. I'd always thought this was a "chick flick" for some reason. Oddly enough it was my wife who informed of the greatness. Watched it a few years ago and loved it.

5. Pretty in Pink (1986) – What? Another missed John Hughes movie? I'd always heard tales of the Ducky character but just never had interest. My bad. Loved what an ass Spader is in this as well.

Movie Characters I'm Likely to Name a Child After (C) Bonus

1. Snake Plissken – Escape From New York (1981) – He'd probably be a real jerk of a kid and naturally he'd have to wear an eye patch.
2. Sloane Peterson – Ferris Bueller's Day Off (1986) – Sloane is on my list of girl's names in case I add to my litter.
3. Chief Martin Brody – Jaws (1975) – Brody was on my list of boy's names...the wife vetoed it. I probably shouldn't have told her about the Jaws connection.
4. Jeffrey Lewbowski – The Big Lewbowski (1998) - He'd have a great nickname already..."The Dude".
5. Axel Foley – Beverly Hills Cop (1984) – My friend Noah totally beat me to it and named his son Axel. Kid's got a bright future!

Movies to Watch While Folding Laundry (C) Bonus

1. Overboard (1987) – Who doesn't love this movie? If you don't...you better check yourself...before you wreck yourself. Kurt obviously rules, but this is my top Goldie movie for sure. This is a movie that is always on TV as well, so next time you're folding laundry...look for it. This is such a fun movie but when you get down to it Kurt Russell basically kidnaps Goldie. God bless the 80's.
2. Bird on a Wire (1990) – I didn't mean to put two Goldie movies on here, but oh well. Bird on a Wire is an underrated 90's flick in my opinion, with an amazing Aaron Neville tune on the soundtrack and a great final scene that takes place in a zoo. I feel like more movies should end in zoos. I love seeing bad guys getting mauled by animals. Mel and Goldie don't have the chemistry Kurt and Goldie do but still an enjoyable film.
3. Dude Where's My Car? (2000) – Big time guilty pleasure. Saw this in theaters with a group of friends back in the day and I alone walked away loving it. I'm

not a big Ashton Kutcher guy but him and Stifler are pretty awesome in this mindless comedy. It's weird that Jennifer Garner was in this. A great minor role by Andy Dick.

4. Short Circuit (1986) – "Number Five is alive." This was such a cool movie as a kid. Johnny Five was so damn funny. As I watch it later in life I wouldn't say it is bad now but definitely not as funny. Also it just feels right having a Guttenberg movie in the book.

5. Over the Top (1987) – This movie has three things that remind me of the 80's: 1) Stallone 2) Arm Wrestling Truckers 3) Kenny Loggins music. Let's be honest we only liked this movie as kids due to the arm wrestling storyline. The kid angle was super lame and Robert Loggia was unnecessarily evil. Meet me halfway...across the sky...

Movie Podcasts (C) Bonus

1. Awesome 80's Podcast – A very entertaining podcast where hosts Lawrence and Michael walk us through some of their favorite 80's films. They cover the classics and the more obscure. Luke and I actually stumbled into Lawrence and Michael at a random New Orleans restaurant while we were visiting for Wrestlemania 30. I consider these guys friends, so check them out.

2. How Did This Get Made? – Paul Scheer, the beautiful June Diane Raphael and Jason Mantzoukas watch movies new and old where they essentially make fun of them. The films are typically regarded as "bad" films but from time to time they uncover a gem. Seems like a simple concept but I promise you it is hilarious. I've grown to love their Live shows the most, in fact I'm going to a Live show in 2018!

3. Now Playing Podcast – Stumbled across these guys while searching for a Friday the 13th podcast probably like 5 years ago. These guys specialize in retrospective

series where they cover all the films in a franchise. The hosts are pretty entertaining and always informative. Check it out.

4. Squared Circle Cinema – A newer listen for me and a great concept. They watch movies featuring professional wrestlers and then chat about them...among other things. Even though they blasted Escape from New York (1981) and I wanted to throat punch them for it...I've looked past it because they are pretty entertaining.

5. Projection Booth Podcast – This is the safest for work of the bunch. Very in-depth look at films. Very informative. These guys really do their homework and often interview folks that worked on the films they cover. Not the most exciting but very good info!

7. Through the Years

We will now take you on a journey back in time...all the way to the 1960's. The journey begins with our favorite movies of the 60's and 70's, then starting in 1980 we give you our top 5 movies in each year from 1980 to 2017. "Where we're going we don't need roads."

(C) = Casey
(L) = Luke

Movies from the 1960's (C)

1. The Magnificent Seven (1960) – Great film with a killer main score. Well I guess it's great if you're into westerns. This film features a phenomenal cast: Yul Brynner, Steve McQueen, Charles Bronson and James Coburn. It's also fun to watch knowing Yul and Steve hated each other during filming. The 2016 remake with Denzel and Chris Pratt was respectable.

2. Batman (1966) – I think jokey Batman is just as good as serious Batman. All just depends on your frame of mind. But I love the Adam West version just as much as the Michael Keaton version. Grew up on this one and I quote it often...typically no one catches my reference. "Some days you just can't get rid of a bomb."

3. The Ghost and Mr. Chicken (1966) – "That a boy Luther!" I remember watching this before summer swim lessons in my youth. And I was immediately intrigued due to 1) Don Knotts 2) a supernatural element 3) a guy keeps yelling "That a boy Luther." Very fun movie! Check it out, classic Don Knotts.

4. McLintock! (1963) – I'm a big John Wayne guy. This is arguably his most fun film. Oddly enough there is no real antagonist, or at least no evil bad guy.

5. The War Wagon (1967) – John Wayne and Kirk Douglas team up for a classic Western. This is weird but the thing I loved most about this movie was Lomax's outfit.

Movies from the 1960's (L)

1. The Dirty Dozen (1967) - Not just a war movie for me, THE war movie that led to my fascination with the genre. I remember my dad watching this with me and filling in the blanks for me when the story got a little too heavy or deep. I still hate seeing Jim Brown go down. He was so close!

2. Magnificent Seven (1960) - One of the granddaddies of them all as far as westerns goes. One of the early great ensembles. I can't really bring myself to watch the new one obviously.

3. Swiss Family Robinson (1960) - I just couldn't believe this story as a youngster. It blew my mind and I started preparing myself for that fateful day when I too, would be stranded on an island with my family. Thank God that didn't happen, we wouldn't have lasted long.

4. Parent Trap (1961) - I see a trend here. All of our VHS tapes were just family movies recorded from the previous decades. A favorite of my sister's that we inevitably watched too much. How dare Lindsay Lohan soil the good name of the Parent Trap?

5. Once Upon a Time in the West (1968) - Discovered this about 40 years after the fact. A great overlooked western. How awesome is that opening sequence? So different and you really could cut the tension with a knife. I also love the fact that the hero is simply named Harmonica.

Movies from the 1970's (C)

1. Jaws (1975) - I saw this very early in life and was mesmerized/terrified. To this day I'm obsessed with sharks...like I watch every single shark documentary on Shark Week. I'm also still terrified of open water. There is something so terrifying about a great white lurking under the water. Story + Sharks + Characters = A+ Movie. "Smile you son of a bitch."

2. Alien (1979) – My personal favorite film in the Alien franchise is the original. The alien is pretty terrifying. Loved the true horror feel of this one. Great cast and the chest bursting scene is so iconic.

3. Star Wars (1977) – I don't think I need to spend much time on this one. Everyone and their mother knows about Star Wars.

4. Dawn of the Dead (1978) – Do you love zombie movies? How about movies that take place in a mall? If you answered yes to both, check this one out.

5. Chisum (1970) – Always loved this John Wayne western because it featured the infamous Billy the Kid. Might be my favorite John Wayne flick of all time.

Movies from the 1970's (L)

1. A New Hope (1977) - I spent 15 minutes the other night watching trailers for The Last Jedi (2017). Almost 30 years after this movie changed the film landscape forever. A trendsetter that laid the foundation for one of the best stories still being told.

2. The Sting (1973) - I came across this movie way too late in life. Awesome stuff. I just want to hang out with Robert Redford and Paul Newman after seeing this. I am actually surprised some studio hasn't redone this one. A great thrilling story.

3. Willy Wonka and the Chocolate Factory (1971) - We had only a few VHS videos growing up. This was one of them and I couldn't come close to giving you an accurate estimate on how many times I watched it. Even as a kid, I remember thinking that the kids other than Charlie were terrible human beings. Iconic character in Willy Wonka and Gene Wilder nailed it.

4. Carrie (1976) - I actually enjoy the horror genre from back in the day. This was story driven and wasn't a brainstorming session of "How gross can we make murder?", like many movies today. Sissy Spacek was awesome. They should show this in schools today and tell the bullies they have a 70% of being burned alive at a formal.

5. Apple Dumpling Gang (1975) - One of the other few VHS tapes we had. This was a go to of mine when I was sick as a kid. Man you really appreciate Don Knotts when you get older.

Movies from 1980 (C)
1. The Private Eyes (1980) – An underrated gem starring Don Knotts and Tim Conway. It's sort of a Sherlock Holmes parody with Knotts and Conway as the two bumbling detectives. I watched this with my dad a lot growing up…like a lot. Knotts and Conway are fantastic together and this is a fun movie. There are so many folks that haven't seen it and that makes me want to cry.
2. Caddyshack (1980) - One of the greatest "sport" movies of all time. Such a quotable movie. All-star cast, even though I find Danny super annoying. Dangerfield, Murray, Chase and others really made this a comedy classic. That gopher dancing to Kenny Loggins at the end will always stick with me. "Cinderella story, outta nowhere."
3. The Empire Strikes Back (1980) – I think this may be the best complete Star Wars film except for the Phantom Menace (1999)…said the liar. Phantom Menace sucks. Empire Strikes Back seems the darkest and I like that. Also there are no Ewoks.
4. Blues Brothers (1980) "We're on a mission from God." Great comedy mixed with even better music. I remember jamming out to this soundtrack on cassette back in the day. This is one of those movies that gets funnier every time you watch it. John Candy alert.
5. The Fog (1980) – John Carpenter is the master of the low budget horror film. I love everything about this film. The actual fog is terrifying…even without knowing murderous spirits seeking revenge are hiding within. Watching these old Carpenter movies just makes me realize how much I hate all the current day CGI.

Movies from 1980 (L)

1. The Empire Strikes Back (1980) - The best installment of arguably the greatest franchise in film. An awesome movie where the bad guys kick a little butt. Perfectly set up the story for decades to come.

2. The Shining (1980) - The biggest "WTH" movie ever? Maybe. I even watched a documentary on The Shining recently. The beauty perhaps is that no one can really explain the darn thing. I drove by the hotel in Estes Park, CO and it sent chills up my spine!

3. Caddyshack (1980) - I am not a huge Dangerfield guy and saw this movie only once. Still, the premise and one liners are great. A young Murray is also a huge positive. Would probably be better if I have ever played a round of golf in my life.

4. Friday the 13th (1980) - I am not big on where they took this franchise but that first one was incredibly iconic. Can anyone ever look at hockey masks the same way?

5. Airplane (1980) - Another classic comedy probably a bit ahead of its time. Leslie Nielson should have been in his prime in the late 90's to present day. Can you imagine the hilarity?

Movies from 1981 (C)

1. Escape from New York (1981) – Quick summary of this film. One of the greatest actors of all time (Kurt). One of the greatest characters of all time (Snake). One of the greatest scores of all time. Not really sure why but it's my ringtone for when my mom calls me. The supporting cast is phenomenal as well starting with Lee Van Cleef. This movie also has the mood of a lot Carpenter films wrapped up into one. A+ flick.

2. Raiders of the Lost Ark (1981) – The beginning of the Indiana Jones franchise and what most consider to the best. I personally give the Last Crusade (1989) the slight edge but they are both fantastic films. I, much like Indy, do not care for snakes. To me Harrison Ford will always be Indiana Jones first! Suck it Star Wars fans.

3. Stripes (1981) – I consider myself a Bill Murray fan but for whatever reason I didn't see this until the late 90's. It bums me out knowing that Murray and Ramis didn't speak to each other for so long, they were such a great duo. The first half of the movie holds up really well but I don't really enjoy the final act. Shout out to John Candy...RIP.

4. American Werewolf in London (1981) – This is such a fun horror movie...if there is such a thing. A good blend of humor with comedy and an amazing transformation scene. I love the English moor setting for the film and the village people (not "The" Village People).

5. Nighthawks (1981) –First 1981 wasn't that great. I know there are a few others films out there that are beloved but I just probably haven't seen them. Second, Nighthawks is awesome. I stumbled across this one recently. A young Sly Stallone is a conservative cop taking on Rutger Hauer, who is a stone cold terrorist. This movie really shocked me, I was not expecting the level of violence and bleakness. Hauer was straight up terrifying in this role. Lando is in this movie...for the Star Wars nerds out there.

Movies from 1981 (L)

1. Raiders of the Lost Ark (1981) - I mean....this is obvious. I don't have to express my love for Indiana Jones again do I?
2. Stripes (1981) - Looking back, has Bill Murray had one of the best careers ever? The guy is nails. I remember my sister fast forwarding through the shower scene as a youngster so I would be allowed to watch.
3. Escape from New York (1981) - Awesome story with the ruggedly handsome Kurt Russell. I really need to see this one again. It has been too long.
4. The Great Muppet Caper (1981) - As I researched 1981 films, two things became apparent. I haven't seen many movies from 1981 and by God I am still a fanboy of Gonzo and Fozzy Bear. I was so into the Muppets as a kid. The soft spot is still there.
5. Das Boot (1981) - Another movie I desperately need to re-watch. I watched it in high school and was one of the first foreign films I remember taking a chance on. I am not sure I would ever want to ride in a submarine but my goodness do I love me some perilous navy action.

Movies from the 1982 (C)

1. The Thing (1982) - This was a movie I saw at way too young of an age. Which is maybe why I found it so horrifying. I think this is John Carpenter's best film. The tone is perfect and bleak, the practical effects are amazing and the cast is top notch. Kurt Russell rules as Mac. Nice efforts from Keith David and Wilford Brimley as well. This movie is the perfect horror movie from the opening scene of the helicopter chasing the dog to the conclusion. One of my favorite things in life is sitting down with people and showing them this movie for the first time.

2. Fast Times at Ridgemont High (1982) - Watched this for the first time in 2017! I know calm down everyone. I don't know what to say. It just slipped through the cracks. I never had the desire to see it. I knew of the Spicoli character and judged a book by its cover. I had no idea how amazing the movie was. The opening features an 80's mall shot which set the tone for a great experience. This movie also had a little bit of a dark side to it as well which I was not expecting. "Hey you guys had shirts on when you came in here."

3. Blade Runner (1982) – What a great year for film. Blade Runner is an acquired taste. When I first saw this movie when I was maybe 10-12, I was beyond bored. When I came back to it in my 20's...I was more impressed. When I watched it again in my 30's...I really enjoyed it. It's art, not a blockbuster film. A great performance from Rutger Hauer really carries the film. Also people who say that Deckard is a Replicant are no friends of mine (Ridley Scott included).

4. Halloween III: Season of the Witch (1982) - I love that every October 31st the Halloween franchise movies play for at least 24 hours. When I was younger I would always catch bits and pieces of Season of the Witch. However one year I finally found the time to take in all of this one...and I loved it. This is now my favorite of the series even without Michael Meyers. I would argue that Conal Cochran is way more evil than Meyers. This dude wants

to kill every kid in the world. Also the Silver Shamrock jingle is phenomenal. If you don't like this movie I will fight you.

5. Tron (1982) – What a cool movie this was as a kid. I remember seeing this at my neighbor's house and my cousin Johnny had the Nintendo game. It's a great concept of the human getting sucked into the computer...it felt way ahead of its time. Those light cycle scenes will forever stick with me. Going back, the graphics don't seem to hold up but the nostalgia factor is strong with this one. How great was the Tron character? I really wish Tron: Legacy (2010) could have delivered a better sequel.

Movies from 1982 (L)

1. ET (1982) - I mean this movie was a monster (sorta literally). I was scared as a boy but eventually took the plunge. Who remembers the ride at Universal Studios? An iconic character. I have never loved something so ugly before or since.

2. Star Trek II: Wrath of Khan (1982) - We were a Star Trek family. This film was a pretty big deal growing up. Can anyone not yell "KHANNNNN" when thinking about this? If you can, we are not friends.

3. Poltergeist (1982) - This movie scared the bejesus out of me. Still one of the most terrifying movie experiences ever. I somehow found this on TV as a kid when no one was watching. I didn't watch TV for 17 years afterwards.

4. Tron (1982) - Fact: I didn't know this movie existed until 2007. My friend Josh loved it and essentially made me watch it. I signed up on Jeff Bridges alone. A great little film that is pretty overlooked, even after the reboot years later.

5. First Blood (1982) - If you were a boy in the 1980's, Rambo was a part of your world. I think I have to list this solely based on the sheer number of imaginary bad guys I killed thanks to First Blood.

Movies from 1983 (C)

1. Return of the Jedi (1983) - I love the opening to Jedi. The rescue mission at Jaba the Hut's place is the best. Those damn Ewoks almost ruined the movie though. I admit I enjoyed them as a kid but now I loathe them. Still a great third addition to the Star Wars franchise.

2. Christine (1983) – A dream matchup. A John Carpenter film from Stephen King source material. As a kid I would go over to my buddy Adam's house to watch scary movies. This was one we watched. Enjoyed it the first time I saw it and still enjoy it to this day. Just a well-made film.

3. Vacation (1983) – A Chevy Chase classic. My absolute favorite part is John Candy at the end as the Walley World employee. This is a must see if you haven't already. "Sorry folks, park's closed. Moose out front shoulda told ya."

4. The Outsiders (1983) – 1983 wasn't a great year in film. While I enjoy #4 and #5 they won't be appearing anywhere else in these lists. My eighth grade teacher read the book to us in school which heightened my interest...then I watched the movie. Holy cow what a cast. Movie is only solid but it's good to see Swayze, Cruise, Estevez and the crew all on screen together. "Stay Gold Ponyboy."

5. Jaws 3 (1983) – Big fan of the Jaws franchise...even though this movie is far from great. I enjoy seeing young Dennis Quaid and Lea Thompson, while Louis Gossett Jr. takes the cake for his boisterous performance. The scene where the shark breaks the control room glass is so terrible looking that I used to rewind it like 20 times to watch it. Hated those dolphins too! No way they stop a great white shark!

Movies from 1983 (L)

1. Return of the Jedi (1983) - Emotional. A good end to the Star Wars story. Looking back, the Ewoks were hokey but they were adorable as a kid. Darth Vader finally turning back to the good side literally made me cry as a child.
2. Vacation (1983) - There is literally no family vacation I take where I don't at least give this movie a passing thought. As an avid planner, I can't imagine the Walley World experience. Makes the movie stick out to me even more.
3. Trading Places (1983) - One of those comedies where I had to watch the TV or edited version but still! Two SNL greats in one of their best performances. Life lessons and laughter in one movie.
4. War Games (1983) - LOVED this. I remember watching this at least four times with my good friend Nick. It also kind of scared me but of course I was too cool to admit that. I vividly remember this being one of the movies we would always watch at his dad's house.
5. Scarface (1983) - This movie is terribly overrated. There I said it. It is only here because it is decent and I apparently didn't partake in many 1983 films. The pop culture fascination with the movie is annoying to me. Deal with it.

Movies from 1984 (C)
1. Beverly Hills Cop (1984) – "Look man I ain't falling for no banana in the tailpipe." One of the best movies to ever come out of Hollywood. Eddie Murphy was absolute perfection in the role of Axel Foley. In case you care the Axel F theme is my ringtone.
2. Ghostbusters (1984) – "Who ya gonna call?" Bill Murray at his finest. This has been such a classic...from the Stay Puft Marshmallow Man to Rick Moranis. Also the Ghostbusters theme song is one of my kid's favorite songs (mine as well). "I gotta split the mayor wants to rap with me about some things."
3. Gremlins (1984) – Ah the 80's when movies were billed as kids' movies even though they clearly weren't. I first saw this when I was little, like way too little to be watching a movie about murderous little gremlins. Gizmo was such an adorable little guy though wasn't he? I used to have a record/book combo when I was little that I would listen to before bed and it freaked me out. Also my son is begging me to let him see this...keep in mind Lion King is too scary for him.
4. Sixteen Candles (1984) – I was late to the party on Sixteen Candles. Not sure how this slipped by, I've always been a big John Hughes fan. I'd always thought this was a "chick flick" for some reason. Oddly enough it was my wife who informed of the greatness. Watched it a few years ago and loved it.
5. Police Academy (1984) – Another big hit in the Heaton household, we watched the Police Academy films interchangeably. Guttenberg's "one in the oven" shirt absolutely kills me. Michael Winslow's sound effects were the coolest thing on planet Earth when I watched this as a kid.

Movies from 1984 (L)

1. Ghostbusters (1984) - My 7 year old just asked me recently if I had seen this. The fact that kids are asking their dad's about this 34 years later is a testament to its awesomeness. Is there anything wrong with this one? Also one of the few times where I tolerated Rick Moranis. Sorry Canada.
2. Temple of Doom (1984) - It was hard not giving Mr. Jones the number one spot here. The scene where the guy reaches into the man to remove his heart is etched in my mind in a terrified youngster kind of way.
3. Footloose (1984) - Kevin Bacon on the scene. This song is still a wedding reception staple. Just reading the synopsis and you would bet this movie sucked. It didn't, it excelled. Let's Daaaaaaance.
4. Beverly Hills Cop (1984) - Axel Foley (insert funny laugh here). I remember even my parents getting into this one. I loved it, pretty sure I was too young to be watching it but I remember us owning the VHS and it got a lot of tread at the Worrell house.
5. Karate Kid (1984) - I believe it was federal law to watch and adore this movie if you were male and alive in the 1980's.

Movies from 1985 (C)

1. Clue (1985) – My sister and I watched Clue so many times as kids it was silly. Clue has to be the best movie based on a board game...except for maybe Battleship...psych! Battleship was horrible and Clue rules. Tim Curry is great in this but Mr. Green steals the show. My sister and I would always play a game about who we would recast in a remake...I guess Hollywood didn't get our suggestions. "They all did it. Now I'm going to go home and sleep with my wife."

2. Teen Wolf (1985) – Grew up on this one. Some terribly awesome basketball action in this one. Great music and montages. Stiles is one of the greatest characters of any film and I love his t-shirts. One thing that always bothered me is that Michael J. Fox didn't play the championship game as the wolf. What a dummy. Also terrible officiating...they let that dickhead stand directly under the basket whilst MJF shoots his free throws.

3. Back to the Future (1985) – Back to back MJF! And yes I put Teen Wolf over the BTTF...deal with it. I will acknowledge that BTTF is the better made movie in every aspect. And it has a wonderful Huey Lewis cameo. BTTF remains a timeless classic to this day. "Hello! McFly! Anybody home?"

4. Fletch (1985) – Underrated Chevy Chase flick. Other than maybe Christmas Vacation (1989), this has to be Chevy's funniest role. I feel like Chevy tries too hard in a lot of his films but Fletch just seemed to flow magically. Chevy wise-cracking at his finest. This movie also inspired a burrito at Moe's.

5. Breakfast Club (1985) – I remember watching this movie for the first time with my older cousins and thinking I was so damn cool. Is this what high school was like in the 80's? In my mind...yes. John Hughes nailed it. What iconic characters. "Grab some wood bub."

Movies from 1985 (L)

1. The Goonies (1985) - I remember seeing the VHS case at Stars and Stripes Video and immediately being drawn to it. This movie was made for kids and still holds up. I have to get Kale to watch this soon. They also made a Nintendo game out of this which added to its lore and legend. Sloth, Chunk, One Eyed Willie. LOVE it. I also yell "Andy......You Goooooonie" in a very cheesy way on an annual basis.

2. Back to the Future (1985) - If I ask you to name the best film series of the 80's? It has to be this or Indiana Jones right? The concept was done and no one else could have played these characters. Great casting on top of the obvious.

3. Clue (1985) - I kid you not, my sister and I rented this to the point where our parents should have just bought it. This movie led to "Clue" being the board game of choice in our house. Mind you, I was probably age five to nine when we played so I lost every time and yet it still didn't ruin the movie for me. Mrs. Peacock in the kitchen with the rope. You heard it here first...

4. Rocky IV (1985) - Perhaps we need Sly Stallone to head over to Russia now and smooth things over? If it worked on Drago, it might work on Putin. The buildup of Drago was amazing. I think this is probably the Rocky movie that guys my age immediately think of because Ivan was so imposing.

5. The Witness (1985) - I came across this later in life but a very solid movie. Harrison Ford was gold back then. Love the story too. Not every movie you get to see a guy murdered in a grain bin and I am an Ag guy so...

Movies from 1986 (C)

1. Big Trouble in Little China (1986) – Another John Carpenter classic. Jack Burton is one of my all-time favorite characters and he some fantastic lines in this. Kurt steals the show but some great performances by Victor Wong (the Grandpa in 3 Ninjas) and James Hong (he is the Asian Samuel L. Jackson, meaning he has been in like 1 million movies). Also for you Sex and the City fans... Samantha is in this. If you haven't see this please take the proper steps to do so. "May the wings of liberty never lose a feather."

2. The Golden Child (1986) – I always think of this movie as being a companion piece to Big Trouble in Little China. They came out in the same year, they both have the strong mystical Asian influence, they are both hilarious and they both have Victor Wong and James Hong. Very underrated film, go support Eddie. Great opening song by Ann Wilson: "The Best Man in the World".

3. Transformers: The Movie (1986) – Watched Transformers the cartoon movie for the first time at my neighbor's house not long after it came out. I was young and a huge Transformers fan. Watching the on screen death of Optimus Prime tore me up as a kid. I was in total shock. I didn't even pay attention for the rest of the film. It was a very sobering walk home. Once I got over the initial shock I went back to the film and actually enjoyed it. Great soundtrack featuring Stan Bush.

4. Top Gun (1986) – Quintessential 80's movie. Great cast, great visuals and great soundtrack. Honestly the coolest thing about this movie was the pilot's nicknames. I still to this day will respond to Iceman if you call me that. "You can be my wingman anytime."

5. Pretty in Pink (1986) – John Hughes put out nothing but hits in the 80's and this is certainly one of them. It's the cliché 80's flick: does the girl choose her goofy

friend or the good looking rich kid? Or at least that's what I thought originally. After actually watching the movie it's so much more. James Spader rules in this.

Movies from 1986 (L)
1. Ferris Bueller's Day Off (1986) - If you had asked me as a kid to rank this year, it wouldn't be #1 but slowly becomes a classic as you get older and understand some of the issues young Mr. Bueller and Cam were dealing with. Timeless really.
2. Crocodile Dundee (1986) - We couldn't get enough of Mr. Dundee. I have never been to Australia but if everyone isn't like Mick, then I probably don't want to go.
3. Top Gun (1986) - Best Tom Cruise movie? Could be. If you didn't cry or get choked up when Goose died, then you are a cold-hearted robot. Also when you are young and a movie is about fighter jets, then everything else is gravy.
4. The Labyrinth (1986) - Jennifer Connelly is gorgeous. I didn't know that then but I do now. I also know that this was a creepy movie and David Bowie freaking hit it out of the park. I still sing this soundtrack on a monthly basis.
5. Stand by Me (1986) - One of the first movies I ever remember being really emotional about. Something about this story of young friends against the odds and on an adventure was compelling. The epilogue portion left me with a lump in my throat. One of my first encounters with this.

Movies from 1987 (C)
1. Beverly Hills Cop 2 (1987) - Just as funny as the original. Eddie is pure gold. They assembled basically the same cast with the addition of Brigitte Nielsen and a Chris Rock cameo. "Y'all both look like Gerald Ford."
2. Adventures in Babysitting (1987) – Another film frequently rented by my family. I've already mentioned the healthy crush I had on Elisabeth Shue. Just an all-around great film, can't wait to show my kids this one. It's hilarious to watch now and see D'Onofrio as a young skinny Thor. Cracks me up.
3. Predator (1987) – Arnold at his finest. He and Carl Weathers share the manliest "hand shake" in cinema history. Fantastic performance from Jesse "The Body" Ventura as well. Got the old time theater in my town to show this as one of the Friday Night Late Shows. "Dillon, you son of a bitch."
4. The Princess Bride (1987) – I've come to love this movie more and more as I get older. I remember liking it when I was younger but nowhere near the level I do now. For instance when I first saw this all I cared about was Andre the Giant being in the movie…but now I can appreciate the rest. Also how awesome was Fred Savage's bedroom at the beginning. He was representing some He-Man, Captain America, Walter Payton, The Fridge and Judge Dredd. "As you wish."
5. The Untouchables (1987) – When I picture Al Capone in my mind I see Robert De Niro. This is a great film with some power players of the 80's. De Niro, Costner and Connery. A classic 80's film I remember watching with my dad and not fully understanding why people couldn't drink booze.

Movies from 1987 (L)

1. The Adventures in Babysitting (1987) - Another staple of ours growing up. I didn't quite get most of the jokes but it really got funnier as I got older. This movie was so 1980's but I still love it. Now as a grown man, I also see why Elizabeth Shue appealed to the dad crowd.

2. Can't Buy Me Love (1987) - I think kids today need to watch movies from the 1980's. All of life's lessons right here….on grainy VHS tapes. Another movie that I enjoyed more and more as the years go by.

3. The Untouchables (1987) - Costner in addition to a historical storyline? Where do I sign up? I am fairly certain I didn't know or appreciate Sean Connery when I first saw this either.

4. Empire of the Sun (1987) - A troubling emotional movie. True story, Casey and I were in college and driving to Kansas for a little trip. The song (that's all I need to say for those who have seen it) came on…I think we didn't speak for 90 minutes and just reflected on life. It is that kind of movie.

5. Three Men and a Baby (1987) - This movie makes me think about my grandparents. They thought this story was hysterical. I remember watching this and its sequel down on the farm with them. Cheesy little movie but special to me.

Movies from 1988 (C)

1. Die Hard (1988) – Yippee-ki-yay MoFo. I think I've already professed my love for this film trilogy and the John McClane character. Good blend of action and humor. Alan Rickman is on point as the villain. Also nice to see Carl Winslow from Family Matters in a small role. "Come out to the coast, we'll get together, have a few laughs."

2. They Live (1988) – This movie is legit fantastic. Pro wrestling legend, Roddy Piper, is so damn good in this movie and has one of the best lines in Cinema History. The film also features an amazing fight sequence between Piper and Keith David. Also its John Carpenter folks. "I have come here to do 2 things…"

3. Big (1988) – Pre 90's Tom Hanks is one of the greatest things since sliced bread. I like to refer to 80's Tom as the funny years. This is a great story where a 13 year old wishes to grow up and figures out the harsh realities of being an adult. I've actually been looking for a Zoltar machine to become a kid again.

4. The Great Outdoors (1988) – I have very fond memories of this movie. This was a frequently rented movie in the Heaton household. Who doesn't love John Candy? Answer: Trick question. Everyone loves John Candy. I love those talking raccoons.

5. Coming to America (1988) – The Prime of Eddie Murphy's career. A classic tale of a fish out water. The best character in the entire film as to be Randy Watson. "Give a hand to my band, Sexual Chocolate."

Movies from 1988 (L)

1. Willow (1988) - When the old Holliday Inn in Jacksonville was still around, I would occasionly play in the arcade. My favorite game...Willow. When I realized this game was based off of a movie, my mind literally blew out of my head. I even still call our office manager Cindy, "Willow", from time to time just to be mean about her being short.

2. Big (1988) - Early Tom Hanks was sensational and this was a great movie with a lot of lessons. Now as an adult, I wish I could find a way to become a kid again. Then again a sequel called "Small" probably would have sucked.

3. Rain Man (1988) - This might have come out in 1988 but I don't think I watched it until about 2008. Good grief what a movie. That young and dastardly handsome Tom Cruise was a great pairing with the true gem of the movie, Dustin Hoffman's Raymond Babbitt.

4. Crocodile Dundee 2 (1988) - While it doesn't match the original, Crocodile Dundee was big in the Worrell home in the late 1980's. We even taped both to VHS somehow. I would often play "Crocodile Dundee". I don't remember what that really entailed but I imagine it got me in trouble frequently.

5. Short Circuit 2 (1988) - I am learning that 1988 was one of two things. One...a year that I didn't see a lot of movies from , two...a year where movies sucked. Not sure how this sequel makes the cut but my sis and I were huge marks for Johnny Five. We wore out Prestige video's copies of both Short Circuit (1986) and Short Circuit 2.

Movies from 1989 (C)

1. Major League (1989) – This a film I quote on a daily basis. I remember my dad had recorded this onto VHS from HBO back in the day and I freakin' loved it. I played baseball my whole life and I'd like to think I'm funny so this movie was right in my wheelhouse. "Look at this effin guy."

2. Tango and Cash (1989) – Kurt and Stallone on the same screen? That's a little piece of heaven right there. Is this the best Buddy Cop movie of all time? That's debatable. Does it have the best high five ending in cinema history? Easily. It's a must watch for the legendary high five alone. There's also a teachable moment surrounding electricity and rain for you scholars of the world.

3. Indiana Jones and the Last Crusade (1989) – This is going to be unpopular with the masses, but this is my favorite Indiana Jones movie. I enjoy this one over Raiders, but most likely because I was seven when I first saw this. Fun Fact: The Indiana Jones theme is my dad's ringtone to this day.

4. Batman (1989) – Best Batman movie and Keaton is the best Batman...no brainer. Nicholson is the better Joker in my book but I'll admit Ledger was pretty amazing as well. "Ever dance with the devil in the pale moon light?" Fun Fact: this was the first movie I ever saw in a movie theater.

5. Field of Dreams (1989) – This was a big hit in my household. Probably in my dad's top 10 of all time. Costner ruled in this era. And yes I have been to the actual Field of Dreams field in Dyersville IA. "Ease his pain."

Movies from 1989 (L)

1. Field of Dreams (1989) - Baseball? Check. Kevin Costner at the height of his powers? Check. Pure emotion? Check. Memorable performances and quotes? Check. This movie literally has everything I could want. It's impact has only grown on me now that I am a father to two boys.

2. Glory (1989) - I am a Civil War buff. I could just end there and feel this placement is justified. This was also Denzel Washington's coming out party and only adds to the legend that is Morgan Freeman. I still get "broken jaw" syndrome where I try not to tear up.

3. Christmas Vacation (1989) - Few movies become "traditions" but this movie in December is like putting up a stocking. You kinda just have to do it. It holds up and is a timeless classic.

4. Back to the Future 2 (1989) - One of the first grownup movies I remember seeing in the theaters. A rare occurrence where a sequel doesn't miss a beat. I remember the cliff hanger to this day. Sentimental memories for me to this day.

5. Indiana Jones and the Last Crusade (1989) - I love me some Indy. Indy + Sean Connery works for me. Incredibly hard to pick just 5 out of 1989. I can't believe the titles that year. Archeology still fascinates me and it all started with this series.

Movies from 1990 (C)

1. Dick Tracy (1990) – Love this movie. Saw it in theaters when I was eight and was totally mesmerized. I love the look of this film, it's so visually pleasing to me. This is going to sound crazy but this is my favorite Al Pacino performance. I have a tie-in book that I got at the school book fair back in 1990 that I still read to my kids to this day.

2. Tremors (1990) – One of those movies that was always on TV it seemed like. Just an all-around fun movie. Also it has Steven Keaton from Family Ties. Fred Ward and Kevin Bacon appeared to be having a great time while working on this film.

3. Young Guns 2 (1990) – I've always liked the sequel better and that is only because of Arkansas Dave Rudabaugh played by Christian Slater.

4. Kindergarten Cop (1990) – "It's not a tumor." I've probably not seen this in 20 years but it holds a high nostalgia factor in my mind. At eight years old this was probably my first Arnold flick.

5. Men at Work (1990) – Guilty pleasure. Super dumb movie BUT I love it. Real life bro's Emelio Estevez and Charlie Sheen play slacker garbage men...you're already hooked right? Everyone should see this.

Movies from 1990 (L)

1. Dances with Wolves (1990) - This movie is so dang emotional. Costner at his peak, in a time piece right up my alley. I watched this a couple times and honestly a part of me never wants to go through the emotional toll of seeing it again. One of the first "grown up" movies I saw that really affected me.

2. Home Alone (1990) - Timeless classic. Not even Macaulay Culken's current state can ruin this for me. I will be especially careful when traveling to Paris with my family.

3. The Hunt for Red October (1990) - Freaking money. The best non-Bond Connery film? Could be. A super skinny Alec Baldwin is a positive as well. The best of several really good submarine movies.

4. Ghost (1990) - Heaven help 1990. How someone watched all of these titles and wasn't in a depressive emotional coma is beyond me. Ghost has many timeless quotes and scenes that people reference 27 years later. I dare someone to make pottery and not think about Ghost....can't happen.

5. Pretty Woman (1990) - "Princess Vivian! Princess Vivian!" A great movie and perhaps one of the best romantic comedies of all time with several super serious undertones. I also feel for actual prostitutes in 1990. Not only for the sad state of their profession but on top of that, they were expected to look like a young Julia Roberts.

Movies from 1991 (C)

1. Terminator 2: Judgment Day (1991) - T2 is actually better than the original. And don't get it twisted, I really like the first one. I loved Arnold being the bad ass in the first one but man I think he is even better as the good terminator In T2. Another highlight is the T-1000. Such a great villain, he felt unstoppable at times. One minor complaint is Edward Furlong...enough said. Also to be noted, Bobby Budnick from "Salute Your Shorts" has a small part.

2. Teenage Mutant Ninja Turtles II: Secret of the Ooze (1991) – My favorite Ninja Turtles movies. I love the tone of this movie. It's definitely the funniest of the turtle films. Also, it features my guys Ernie Reyes Jr. and Vanilla Ice. "Go Ninja, Go Ninja, Go"

3. Robin Hood Prince of Thieves (1991) – Saw this one in theaters with my family back in the day. We were all big Costner fans and who doesn't love a Robin Hood story? But honestly my favorite thing about this movie is the Bryan Adams companion song. (Everything I Do) I Do It For You. To be noted, Alan Rickman was a great Sheriff of Nottingham.

4. Point Break (1991) – Johnny Utah...what a great character name. Swayze is the best part of this movie, though I find just about everyone entertaining...even Gary Busey. "Utah, get me two."

5. Backdraft (1991) – The best fire fighter movie right? Has to be. Last year during my work's fire drills I called a fire fighter "Bull McCaffrey"...he did not appreciate my joke. Also there is a rooftop party scene where Billy Baldwin's hair is being blown every which way by gusts of winds. Must see.

Movies from 1991 (L)

1. Robin Hood: Prince of Thieves (1991) - The fact that Casey nails Duncan's "They took my eyes." line is honestly enough for me here. What else I can say is that Kevin Costner and Morgan Freeman in 1991 were a freaking dream. Easily one of my top 25 favorite movies.

2. Silence of the Lambs (1991) - I definitely wasn't watching this as a nine year old but when I got around to seeing this, my mind was blown. Is there a more iconic villain than Hannibal Lecter? Or is he even a villain at all? The poor guy who played Buffalo Bill can't do anything anymore without me cringing at this sight.

3. What about Bob? (1991) - I feel like this movie gets some unwarranted hate. Bill Murray was sensational and I find myself coming back to this movie over and over. "Roses are red, violets are blue, I'm a schizophrenic and so am I."

4. Hook (1991) - Unbelievably fun movie. Tiny Julia Roberts, Dustin Hoffman as Hook, Robin Williams in his best non-Mrs. Doubtfire role. All the makings of a classic.

5. The Rocketeer (1991) - I remember seeing this in the theaters with "Big Al" Allan Worrell. I was captivated from the beginning. One of the theater experiences I remember the most as a child. I wonder how many broken bones boys suffered in 1991 after seeing this movie…

Movies from 1992 (C)

1. Wayne's World (1992) – One of my all-time favorites. I remember watching this for the first time at my buddy David's birthday party. The Bohemian Rhapsody scene is one of the greatest scenes in cinema history. I quote this movie at least once a day.

2. Under Siege (1992) – Not a big Seagal fan BUT this movie rules! It should also be said I support characters named Casey. Gary Busey did a great job of "playing" a crazy person. This film also put Tommy Lee Jones on the map for me.

3. A Few Good Men (1992) – "Did you order the Code Red?" (I feel that was a joke a Taco Bell worker dropped on me, back when they still carried Mt. Dew Code Red) Great film and cast. I think I watched this for the first time in 2011. "You can't handle the truth."

4. 3 Ninjas (1992) – A guilty pleasure of mine. This is currently my kid's favorite movie. It's a bit corny now that I'm older but I still can't help but laugh when I see a guy get kicked in the nuts. "Rocky loves Emily."

5. Patriot Games (1992) – I grew up in a pro-Harrison Ford family. I watched all of his movies with my dad. Who doesn't love the Jack Ryan character?

Movies of 1992 (L)

1. Wayne's World (1992) - My favorite comedy EVER. Has there ever been a comedy more ahead of its time? I kid you not, I quote this movie once a week. How do people live in Aurora while in the shadow of this cinematic giant?

2. A League of their Own (1992) - I have expressed my love for this film in other lists. A great collaborative effort by a diverse cast. I still can't quite figure out how Lori Petty didn't go on to be a huge star. Was it Tank Girl? Was she mean? Was she overshadowed by the bigger names? "Well, I'm a peach."

3. Reservoir Dogs (1992) - Grippingly clever movie. My favorite Tarantino film. So different and so awesome. Troubling and engrossing all in one. I love movies that captivate solely on writing and performance. If you watch this again, notice how few set changes there are. No frills, just great storytelling.

4. Patriot Games (1992) - Harrison Ford hit a home run with his series as "Jack Ryan". The thinking man's action drama is probably my favorite genre and it most likely started with movies like this. This joined with Clear and Present Danger (1994) are insanely good.

5. Last of the Mohicans (1992) - I love this period piece. It is also my first memory of Daniel Day Lewis. Awesome story with a historical backdrop. Soundtrack is epic. I have to fight the urge to attack someone with a tomahawk every time I see it.

Movies from 1993 (C)

1. Tombstone (1993) – Tombstone is always in the rotation for my all-time favorite film. I'm a sucker for a good western and the cast is amazing. Kurt Russell is a good Wyatt, but Val Kilmer steals the show. It's a shame Val didn't win an Oscar for his role as Doc Holliday. At least Val won the MTV Movie Award for Best Male Performance. A lot of other good performances as well but you get the idea.

2. Jurassic Park (1993) –Saw this movie 3 times in theaters I loved it so much. Michael Crichton (RIP) gets a shout out for writing the source material, but Spielberg gets even more credit for bringing JP to life. This movie seemed so real and the CGI was not distracting. If there is a child of the 90's out there that doesn't like JP I would be genuinely flabbergasted. "Clever girl."

3. So I Married an Axe Murderer (1993) – One of my wife's favorite comedies and definitively up there for me as well. This was a big hit in Central Illinois because at the coffee house Meyers stands in front of a map of the U.S. and right above his shoulder is Illinois. It's funny to go back and watch all of Mike's movies and see the bits he reuses throughout his career.

4. Surf Ninjas (1993) – Guilty pleasure of mine. This movie was made and advertised for 11 year olds…which was perfect for me at the time. I recently re-watched Surf Ninjas and I still love it. Leslie Nielsen is a great villain. It's funny because he is doing Naked Gun type shtick but he is also evil and torturing people. Everyone should see this. Oh and Rob Schneider is in it. My co-worker Aaron who was born in 93 loves this movie…which is a miracle he's even heard of it.

5. Demolition Man (1993) – Probably my favorite Stallone flick. I'll never forget watching this for the first time at my buddy James H's house. I instantly fell for

this film. Great role for Sandra Bullock, Wesley Snipes is entertaining AND...Taco Bell is the only surviving fast food restaurant. Did anyone ever figure out the physics of the seashells? I'd like to know.

Movies from 1993 (L)

1. Gettysburg (1993) - I've proven my love for this film many a time in this little book. Besides Tom Berenger's hideously fake beard, there isn't anything not to love for me.

2. Tombstone (1993) - The best western ever? I could argue that. I am 35 and still want to be Val Kilmer's Doc Holliday when I grow up...expect for the terrible health and early death of course.

3. The Fugitive (1993) - What a freaking year 1993 was. I am praying that one day I see a physician with the last name of Kimble. I will have a field day with the cheesy one-liners. Tommy Lee Jones's best role in my opinion and that says a lot.

4. Jurassic Park (1993) - I honestly was a little scared to see this movie. Like legit scared. I didn't think I was quite ready to see people eaten by dinosaurs, but it turns out I could watch people get eaten by dinosaurs. Great movie that the subsequent sequels couldn't replicate.

5. Groundhog Day (1993) - Bill Murray is a mad genius. This is the type of movie that keeps improving over time and I never view February 2nd the same anymore. Chris Elliot with a nice little addition here. I also can't take anyone named Phil seriously.

Movies from 1994 (C)

1. Ace Ventura Pet Detective (1994) – Hey it's the crazy guy from In Living Color. One of the all-time great quotable movies. Such a great film and no one saw this one coming. This is a movie I can watch anytime. I'm also not embarrassed to admit I liked Tone Loc...as a kid. "Hi I'm looking for Ray Finkle...and a clean pair of shorts."

2. Dumb and Dumber (1994) – Strong year for Jim Carrey. Two of his funniest films in the same year. Whenever I come across this on TV I always get sucked in. So many great parts it seems like I find something new each time. Great soundtrack that I owned on CD as a kid. "If that guy over there is Sea Bass."

3. Maverick (1994) – This is funny Mel Gibson at his finest, before he went bonkers. I remember watching this one several times with my dad. I watched it again not long ago and I think I liked it even more. My dad had the soundtrack on cassette and there was a fantastic rendition of "Amazing Grace." Nice little cameo by Danny Glover as well.

4. Clear and Present Danger (1994) – Another Jack Ryan hit. I like this better than Patriot Games (1992). Harrison Ford on top of his game. Saw this in theaters with a good family friend.

5. True Lies (1994) – Great Arnold flick. Love the story of the family man being a secret agent. Jamie Lee Curtis and Tom Arnold are amazing as well. Fun fact: I just purchased this DVD from a lady at work for $1 last week.

Movies from 1994 (L)

1. Shawshank Redemption (1994) - Top 10 movie of all time for me. I can watch this movie again and again and the emotion is there every time. Morgan Freeman and Tim Robbins can't be praised enough for their performances in my opinion. I also love how I couldn't really tell you much about the supporting cast but darn they were all amazing! Cinematic masterpiece.

2. Forest Gump (1994) - I think this is the role Tom Hanks will always be associated with and that is saying a ton. The story being beautifully woven through specific periods in history was a great touch. Gary Sinise should have won two Oscars as Lt. Dan.

3. Dumb and Dumber (1994) - Jim Carrey was untouchable at this time but this was easily his best movie. Also proves the insane diversity that Jeff Daniels is capable of. I think you can ask anyone in their 30's about this movie and they would have vivid memories of it.

4. Clear and Present Danger (1994) - Harrison Ford as Jack Ryan was a match made in heaven. I could watch an aging Harrison Ford play an aging Jack Ryan today and be perfectly happy with it. Willem Dafoe was a great touch and it was an awesome movie experience.

5. Stargate (1994) - I am not normally a big Sci-Fi guy but this movie captivated me. I taped this (old school to a VHS!) during a free HBO trial weekend. My first memory of James Spader is also a nugget worth noting.

Movies from 1995 (C)

1. Ace Ventura When Nature Calls (1995) – Controversial pick here due to the tone of the film. You know what? Deal with it! I love this movie and no one can take that from me. Back when Jim Carrey was funny and not too crazy...those were the days.

2. Tommy Boy (1995) – Another silly movie but c'mon I was 13 in 1995. This movie is a comedy classic. Farley and Spade were magic together. A real bummer to think that just two years later Farley would be dead. I vividly remember eating at a Long John Silver's with Luke and his dad the day he passed.

3. Die Hard with a Vengeance (1995) – What a great installment to the Die Hard franchise. Way better than the second and right on par with the first. This is around the time I started taking notice of Samuel L. Jackson. "No he said Hey...Zeus."

4. Toy Story (1995) – Sentimental pick. I may have been a little too old for this when it came out but that didn't stop me from loving it. I've always loved the idea of toys coming to life. It's such a great concept and Pixar really nailed it. Side note: Have y'all read *Indian in the Cupboard*?

5. Billy Madison (1995) – A gem from back when Sandler was funny. I don't blame Sandler, it's so hard to stay fresh for so long. Humor evolves. I laugh out loud every time I watch this! And I don't give out pity laughs, just ask my wife. "Touch her boob? That's assault brotha."

Movies from 1995 (L)
1. Braveheart (1995) - Quite bluntly, this is my favorite movie of all time so it certainly takes the top spot in 1995.
2. Apollo 13 (1995) - Hall of Fame cast full of great performances. Based on history and accurately portrayed, which happens about as often as the Olympics. The kind of movie you can watch over and over.
3. Tommy Boy (1995) - One of the comedies that defined my teen years. Timeless treasure that only gets better with age. I bet I quote this movie a dozen times a year over 20 years later.
4. Mallrats (1995) - I can't quite explain why but I have always adored this movie. One of the best low budget indies of all time. Made better when you go back and see what a lot of these actors and actresses became. I might actually quote this movie more than I quote Tommy Boy.
5. The Usual Suspects (1995) - Quite possibly the best swerve ending of all time. I remember watching this late one night with Chris B on VHS. We were blown away. You can utter the name Keyser Soze 22 years later and get a noticeable reaction from almost anyone.

Movies from 1996 (C)

1. Black Sheep (1996) – My top true comedy. Yea that's right, I like it even better than Tommy Boy. I still audibly chuckle when I watch this film. My cousin Katie and I frequently quote this one back and forth. Farley and Spade were an A+ comedic duo. Bums me out that Farley left the world so early. "Well it's kind of easy to win when you NEVER MOVE YOUR BACK ROW!"

2. The Rock (1996) – All around fantastic movie. Ed Harris, whilst basically being a terrorist, was a very likeable bad guy. Then you have one of Luke's favorite actors in Nic Cage teaming up with Sir Sean Connery. I don't know what's not to love. More movies should be filmed at Alcatraz. Random shout out to my cousin Sumeet for The Rock being his favorite movie. Godspeed.

3. Mission Impossible (1996) – This is one the whole Heaton family saw in theaters. And even though I hated seeing Emelio go down in the first quarter of the film, I powered through. This was back when I wasn't embarrassed to be a Tom Cruise fan as well. The scene where he dangles from the wires while not triggering the alarms is fantastic. Can't believe this franchise is still going.

4. Scream (1996) – What a cool movie. Scream was way ahead of its time, breaking down the scary movie fourth wall and referencing all the movie tropes. I even liked the following sequels...well most of them. "What's your favorite scary movie?"

5. The Nutty Professor (1996) – "Hercules, Hercules." If only they would make a movie where Eddie Murphy just played like 50% of the characters...that would be really something. Oh wait, that's this movie, and I applaud the move. As much as I love Sherman Klump, I was always more of a Buddy Love guy.

Movies from 1996 (L)

1. A Time to Kill (1996) - This movie makes me feel all the feels. Insanely talented cast puts on a gut wrenching performance. This is the kind of movie where you sit quietly after a viewing and think about life. Such a great drama that I almost always need to follow it up with something that will make me smile.

2. The Rock (1996) - Nicholas Cage will get few mentions by me in this project but this is one of them. This was a great movie for a teenage boy in 1996. Sean Connery is also so awesome that I really started to worry less about getting old after seeing him here.

3. Jerry Maguire (1996) - "Show me the money." " You complete me." I could go on but I will stop. On top of this, you get a Bruce Springsteen song for the soundtrack. What else is there really? I suppose technically this was a sports movie but it is pure emotion wrapped around a great story.

4. Twister (1996) - Fact: I was terrified of tornados growing up. One would think that I would hate this movie but it was great. Hard to see Philip Seymour Hoffman in a bit role but well done. I am still waiting to see cows fly by during a storm.

5. Scream (1996) - One of the few movies where I was worried I might actually pee a little while in the theaters. What a movie experience for a group of teenagers. I loved it.

Movies from 1997 (C)

1. Austin Powers: International Man of Mystery (1997) – Good film but probably my least favorite in the series. '97 was a down year in film in my opinion. I blame Titanic for watering down the movie market. And I always thought that Mrs. Kensington from the 1960's was way hotter than Elizabeth Hurley.

2. The Jackal (1997) – Greatly underappreciated film. Bruce Willis is phenomenal in this flick. Kind of weird seeing Bruce as the bad guy but it works. Richard Gere has a laughable Irish accent in this as well. And if you're ever wanting to see Jack Black get his arm blown off or Bruce kiss another man...this is the film for you!

3. L.A. Confidential (1997) – Great story with a knockout performance by Russell Crowe. Apparently there's a book as well...but the book doesn't have Russ. And circle takes the square.

4. Men in Black (1997) – When Will was still making good movies. I loved the song Will made for the soundtrack and the music video for MTV play. If I had a time machine I would go back to the time when Will Smith was cool. All seemed right with the world.

5. The Man Who Knew Too Little (1997) – Here is a nice little gem not too many people know about. Bill Murray plays the bumbling idiot and stumbles across a real murder. He is fantastic in this and you should see it for Murray's performance alone. His Russian dance at the end is worth the price of admission.

Movies from 1997 (L)

1. L.A. Confidential (1997) - I love this genre. The cast was great and this was before Russell Crowe was a famous Roman gladiator. I re-watched this not all that long ago and it holds up for sure. Kevin Spacey hasn't ruined this one yet.

2. Titanic (1997) - I mean...come on, it was good. I don't care what any guy says. I was set to see this in the theaters with Casey, his girlfriend and another person. We were at the theaters and Casey decided he didn't want to see a 3 hour movie. We weren't old enough to drive and were already there. Casey wanted to wait there for a long time to watch the next viewing of For Richer or Poorer with Tim Allen and Kirstie Alley. I called my sister and she came and picked me up.

3. Contact (1997) - Such an underrated movie. I am not even a huge fan of Jodie Foster but really dug this movie. I rented this from Family Video and then proceeded to make my friends go rent it as well. It was a space science fiction movie done with about 4% of the budget these types of films are given now.

4. Austin Powers (1997) - I am a "Mike Meyers guy". I really remember being underwhelmed by the trailer but gave it a shot based on my love of Wayne Campbell alone. I never in a million years would have guessed it would all lead to a great comedic trilogy. Elizabeth Hurley was pleasant on the eyes and had a great performance as well.

5. Air Force One (1997) - "Get off my plane!" I still say that sometimes while playing airplanes with my son. It is a nice change of pace to see a kick-butt president.

Movies from 1998 (C)

1. The Big Lebowski (1998) – Great flick, "The Dude" is one of the greatest characters in movie history. Also this movie makes me want to go bowling…but just recreational bowling…I don't want to be in a league or anything. "Mark it eight Dude."

2. The Wedding Singer (1998) - Sandler still in his prime and one of the few Drew Barrymore movies I enjoy. This is one movie I could literally watch anytime. "Well I have a microphone and you don't, SO YOU WILL LISTEN TO EVERY DAMN WORD I HAVE TO SAY"

3. BASEketball (1998) - This movie inspired some great games of BASEketball in my friend's driveway. The movie is hilarious but what a genius move combining baseball and basketball. I quote this movie all the time while playing pick-up basketball. "You kids with your loud music and your Dan Fogelberg".

4. The Waterboy (1998) - The Waterboy just brings a smile to my face. It's so dumb but at the same time it's so funny. Saw this in theaters as well, so it kind of holds a special place in my heart (along with 400 other movies).

5. The Man in the Iron Mask (1998) - Caught this one at the theaters back in '98. To be honest, I knew nothing about the film other than Leo was in it. So imagine my excitement when it turned out to be a Three Musketeers movie. Probably my least favorite cast of the Musketeers but you really can't be disappointed with Irons, Malkovich and Depardieu.

Movies from 1998 (L)

1. Saving Private Ryan (1998) - I would take a bullet for Tom Hank's character to survive. This is another movie peppered throughout this book. I can't say enough good things about it. I just DVR'ed it last week. Keep in mind, I own it on DVD. So good that it just seemed like I needed to recognize it in my queue.

2. You've Got Mail (1998) - My wife's favorite movie. I love her watching this movie almost as much as I love it itself. Meg Ryan at the height of her charm. Tom is Tom and you even get some Dave Chappelle screen time.

3. Armageddon (1998) - Ok. This movie is pure cheese. I get it. But I'll be darned if this movie didn't move an immature Luke Worrell in 1998. I had broken jaw syndrome something terrible during that climax.

4. The Truman Show (1998) - Not your typical Carey movie. A great story with so many teachable points. A little ahead of its time considering it was made before the insanity of reality TV. My favorite Carey movie, and any movie with Ed Harris is ok with me.

5. Can't Hardly Wait (1998) - A chick flick movie for the ages. This was a mainstay on those awkward movie nights we all had when we were 15-17 and hanging out with the opposite sex. Also, Jennifer Love Hewitt……my goodness. I had a huge crush on her here.

Movies from 1999 (C)

1. Austin Powers: The Spy Who Shagged Me (1999) – If you can't tell by now I'm a pretty big Mike Myers fan. This was better than the original for sure. I love the evolution of the Dr. Evil character from film to film. Heather Graham was a major babe as well.

2. The Matrix (1999) – Much like Neo, I was not a believer at first. I didn't really mean to, but I didn't see this one in theaters. Finally, after a ton of people told me to check this out...I came to my senses. Instantly loved it. I wish they would have stopped after this one though. Agent Smith was a great villain.

3. The Mummy (1999) – Hopefully this is the only Brendan Frasier movie to make the list. This was a really fun movie. Kind of silly at times but a great popcorn movie. Saw this at the IMAX Theater in Branson, MO which is maybe another reason I had such a great time while watching.

4. Magnolia (1999) – This is one of the weirder movies I enjoy. Great cast including John C. Reilly, Julianne Moore, Phillip Seymour Hoffman, Tom Cruise and William H. Macy. This film also has frogs falling from the sky. I love the Amy Mann song, "Wise Up," featured in the film as well. In summation, you should see this.

5. South Park: Bigger, Longer and Uncut (1999) – South Park the Movie was such a big deal at the time. Obviously the show was a big hit and the movie took it all up 100 notches. The soundtrack is phenomenal and I'm pretty sure they had an Oscar nominated song ("Blame Canada"). When my high school friends and I went to see this, the theater was cracking down on the R rating and not letting under aged kids in (jerks). So we found a random guy about to enter the bar and gave him $5 to pose as our dad so we could get in...only to find the very scenario happen in the movie. Life imitating art...or something like that.

Movies from 1999 (L)

1. The Green Mile (1999) - Another movie that leaves you feeling emotionally drained while dually appreciating the wonderful acting by all. Hanks was Hanks but the supporting cast made this one. I always feel bad when I kill a mouse thanks to this movie.

2. Office Space (1999) - One of the best comedy cult classics of all time. I often fantasize about taking our copier out to an open field and going crazy on it thanks to this movie. Jennifer Anniston was sneaky great in this.

3. 10 Things I Hate About You (1999) - Another movie I immediately associate high school with. This was a great date movie. Funny enough but also had those sweet romantic elements as well. My only problem now is that I feel sad seeing Heath when it comes on TV.

4. Blair Witch Project (1999) - I was all in on the uniqueness here. I remember reading about this in Rolling Stone on vacation. Up until that article, there was that weird suspended reality where some thought this was a true documentary. Thankfully I didn't get crazy motion sick either.

5. Stir of Echoes (1999) - Completely underrated film. I bet I rented this three times from Family Video. The unsung movie of Kevin Bacon's credits. A neat creepy story with a satisfying ending.

Movies from 2000 (C)

1. Gladiator (2000) – This movie still gives me chills. Russ Crowe is the best thing ever in this role. This movie is also the reason I want to throat punch Joaquin Phoenix still to this day. Also to be noted, this is my co-worker and good friend Hak's favorite movie. "Father to a murdered son. Husband to a murdered wife. And I will have my vengeance, in this life or the next."

2. The Patriot (2000) - Watched this one for the first time in a high school history class. I remember running out to the store to buy it that same week. Mel Gibson was on top of the world and Heath Ledger was a rising star...oh how times have changed. Also I'm sure it was somewhat common of the time period but I was a little uncomfortable with Mel hooking up with his dead wife's sister at the end. "Aim small, miss small."

3. Remember the Titans (2000) - "We are the Titans...the mighty mighty Titans!" This movie rules. In fact I've never once come across anyone who ever disliked it. Excellent coaching by Denzel.

4. O Brother, Where Art Thou? (2000) – Even though I feel I need to be in the right mood to watch this movie, I find it very enjoyable. Clooney is fantastic and the soundtrack is unforgettable.

5. Almost Famous (2000) – Almost Famous makes the list due to the killer bus sing-along scene. This film inspired many a Tiny Dancer bus sing-along. I also loved the "Fever Dog" song which was the band's big hit.

Movies from 2000 (L)
1. Gladiator (2000) - In hindsight it is disappointing that this is very historically inaccurate but that doesn't negate the fact that this movie was and is awesome. This was THE movie for me this year. Fun Fact: I ate at Jacksonville's NEW Chinese restaurant "The Best Buffett" right before seeing this movie in the theaters. This was a very big day in my life.
2. Almost Famous (2000) - I love the story and the music. Well done and perhaps the only Kate Hudson movie I have ever liked (Sorry to Ms. Hawn). The bus scene still gets me. A really good coming of age story.
3. Cast Away (2000) - Tom Hanks really can't do anything bad. I really liked it and remember being amazed at how a movie could hook me without hardly any dialogue. A unique and special film. I mean we all cried at a blood-stained volleyball.
4. Memento (2000) - One of those movies where you still aren't exactly sure what you just saw. Does anyone truly know the real story here? A mind bender. A movie where you better be 100% paying attention or you'll get lapped in a second. I like those kind of movies.
5. X-Men (2000) - In all honesty, it isn't the best super hero movie out there but it was the first one that got me really hyped. I was a comic book reader for a period as a boy and "X-Men" was my thing. To see this being made into a big budget movie was really a dream come true for little Luke.

Movies from 2001 (C)
1. Ocean's Eleven (2001) – I just feel cool when I watch this movie. One of the best heist movies out there with an all-star cast. Also, I love how Brad Pitt is constantly eating something in every one of his scenes. I guess you could say he was really chewing the scenery (bad joke).
2. From Hell (2001) - A Jack the Ripper flick with a gritty feel and this was back when Depp was still entertaining. Moral of the story: never accept grapes from a stranger.
3. Moulin Rouge (2001) – Saw this one twice in theaters. The story is solid but the music moves me. The "Elephant Love Medley" gets me jacked up. Hats off to Ewan McGregor for actually singing.
4. Jeepers Creepers (2001) – Fun low budget horror movie. I loved the storyline and the villain is awesome. Great ending and Justin Long isn't too obnoxious. Also, I love that ominous "Jeepers Creepers" tune.
5. Black Hawk Down (2001) - Black Hawk Down gives you a glimpse of urban warfare and it terrifies me. The best part of this movie is the bad ass Eric Bana. I was a huge Eric Bana fan for like one year, then I saw more of his resume.

Movies from 2001 (L)

1. Lord of the Rings: Fellowship of the Ring (2001) - A great piece of this mega huge trilogy that led to many other trilogy's. It all started here and I am forever grateful. Poor Sean Bean...always the heel.

2. Shrek (2001) - I remember this in the theater as well. I never thought an animated movie would be so clever and hysterical. I will forgive Mike Meyers for Love Guru (2008), I have always really loved his work. The whole ensemble nailed it. Fun fact...this also was one of five movies you could watch on a cruise I was on.

3. Oceans 11 (2001) - As much as I didn't like the subsequent films, this was amazing. Great cast! I felt they nailed it at every turn. A fun action and comedy rolled into one. The catchy soundtrack was a big pick up as well. Let's face it...Clooney, Pitt and Damon all in the same movie? Even a heterosexual male can get behind that handsomeness

4. Zoolander (2001) - This is an absolute cult classic and one of my favorite movies to watch with my brother, Casey R. Heaton. We watched this in a Kansas City hotel room and have been quoting it since. I remember I was appalled at the stupidity during the first half of the movie but applauding its genius by the end.

5. Enemy at the Gates (2001) - Granted the story of the Russian/German battle for Stalingrad without any actual Russian or German actors is something you have to look past, but a well done and effective war story with great performances from Ed Harris. One of the first memories I have of Jude Law being a big cinematic player.

Movies from 2002 (C)

1. Lord of the Rings: The Two Towers (2002) – Could have won the Oscar just like Return of the King (2003) did the following year. How bad ass were the Riders of Rohan? The hobbits were testing my nerves in this one though.

2. Austin Powers: Goldmember (2002) – Arguably the best of the series. So many fantastic lines that I still use to this day. Kind of bummed out they teased another sequel that we never got to see. I've also heard rumors of Mike Myers being a turd to work with on the set. "Would you like a shmoke and a pancake?"

3. Sweet Home Alabama (2002) - Factual statement: this is THE BEST romantic comedy in the universe. I don't feel I even need to defend that statement. It's a great plot, it's funny, it's sad, it's gotta little bit of romance...it's gotta a baby in bar. What more do you need? Lightning sculptures? Yea it's totally got that as well. Reese should have retired after making this movie because she reached the pinnacle. This movie also features Patrick Dempsey for you Dr. McDreamy fans out there.

4. Catch Me if You Can (2002) - Incredible film based on a true story about a professional con man. Tom Hanks and Leonardo DiCaprio are fantastic in this movie. They both should have beat Adrian Brody in the Pianist (2002) for the Oscar. Also, I love the name Carl Hanratty.

5. 28 Days Later (2002) – Caught this on HBO after a late night of working back when I was in the minor league baseball biz. I was so enthralled I'm not sure I slept at all. One of my favorite "Zombie" movies. Yes nerds, I know it's the rage virus and not actual zombies.

Movies from 2002 (L)

1. The Bourne Identity (2002) - I honestly didn't have all that high of hopes for this heading into the theater. I was not jacked up but merely going to the theater for something to do. I loved it and it set the ground work for one of my favorite movie franchises.

2. Austin Powers: Goldmember (2002) - A sentimental favorite of mine. I was working at a movie theater at the time so was able to watch it at a special midnight showing. I laughed so hard I nearly cried. The sophomoric humor was killing me which makes sense I guess since I was about to be a sophomore in college.

3. We Were Soldiers (2002) - I liked it so much it was the rare movie that I saw twice in the theaters. Still though....I cringe when I think about the photographer who was gravely wounded by friendly fire. I even stepped outside the theater when I saw it the second time. Give me tough guy Sam Elliot all day long as well please.

4. The Ring (2002) - Honestly, might be the last scary movie that really got me hyped up. I anticipated it greatly and it didn't disappoint. Sentiment is high as well since it was the first movie I ever saw with my wife at the movie theater.

5. Signs (2002) - Ahhhh 2002. We had large Nokia cell phones, shirts from STRUCTURE and M. Night was still making quality movies. Big year for Mel Gibson here apparently. The only blind date I ever went on in my life was to Signs. Ironically, I immediately got a "sign" that she was indeed not the one.

Movies from 2003 (C)

1. Pirates of the Caribbean (2003) – Great story, cast, scenery and music. This is one of those movies that really makes you feel like you're there. Maybe this is why I love the Caribbean so much. Just an all-around fun movie. Captain Jack is an iconic character. Legolas even turns up in this flick.

2. Lord of the Rings: Return of the King (2003) – I'm actually lumping the Two Towers in with this one as well. The Lord of the Rings Trilogy was EPIC. These were movies I struggled to wait for. My cousin Katie was in love Aragorn and sadly, for some reason I'll never be able to forget that.

3. Old School (2003) – My second favorite Will Ferrell movie. This was another movie over quoted on my college campus at the time. I actually heard a Frank the Tank reference at work the other day. If you haven't seen this movie get out from under that rock and check it out. "Snoop, Snoop-a-loop!"

4. Master and Commander (2003) - Saw this with Luke down in South Padre Island. Love me some Russ Crowe. This is probably the best British Navy film ever made.

5. Love Actually (2003) – One of my wife's favorite flicks and for the longest time I pretended to put up with it but then I quit lying to myself. This movie is great. Love all the merging storylines. The obnoxious kid is by far the worst storyline. I'd still put this at #5. "I feel it in my fingers, I feel it in my toes."

Movies from 2003 (L)

1. Mystic River (2003) - Dynamic cast with great emotion. A sad piece but it stays with you. Also an enormous piece of any puzzle when playing "six degrees of Kevin Bacon".
2. Lord of the Rings: Return of the King (2003) - A greatly important trilogy. A wonderful movie theater experience as well. My only knock.....it ended nearly 397 times. I remember thinking I was never going to be allowed to leave the theater.
3. Old School (2003) - A great comedy that really set the stage for Will Ferrell to take the next stage of stardom. Go ahead and take a minute and try to estimate the number of times you've yelled "You're my boy Blue."
4. Pirates of the Caribbean (2003) - The first is usually the best and this is no exception. I remember going in wondering how they were going to pull this off. Was this an action movie or hokey family movie? Somehow they pulled them both off and it was a great movie.
5. Elf (2003) - The Rise of Ferrell. I don't think I appreciated it as much at the time but good grief, it gets better every December when you can find it nightly on TBS.

Movies from 2004 (C)

1. Anchorman (2004) – Another film that I quote every single day. I can't believe this is now 14 years old. Goodnight Irene! Now I feel old. My favorite Will Ferrell role. This was a huge hit during college. I feel like everyone on campus was walking around referencing Anchorman. I also had a thing where I would fall asleep to movies and I fell asleep to this one conservatively 247 times. "Baxter is that you? Bark twice if you're in Milwaukee."

2. King Arthur (2004) – Love the Arthurian Legend and I think this is the best King Arthur movie. We had a buddy who worked at a local theater and he would let us come in after hours for free screenings. King Arthur was one of those free screenings. Clive Owen was a great Arthur but Tristan was by far my favorite character.

3. Man on Fire (2004) – This is the ultimate bad ass Denzel movie. If you are ever traveling to Mexico make sure you take Denzel with you. Dakota Fanning tries her best to ruin this movie but is unsuccessful.

4. Dodgeball (2004) – I feel like this is one of the last movies my family watched together in theaters. My sister was randomly in town and I was in college so it was hard to get us all in the same place at the same time. This was a fun movie centering around one of my favorite PE activities…dodgeball! Fun fact: I played on a dodgeball team in a Church League with Luke.

5. Dawn of the Dead (2004) – Awesome Zombie flick. Much like the original it's set in a mall which is a fantastic setting for a child of the 80's. Some fantastic music in this movie as well. Richard Cheese's cover of "Down with the Sickness" really helps this film get to the next level. If you haven't seen this already…get on it. You'll get to see the dad from Modern Family as well.

Movies from 2004 (L)

1. Anchorman (2004) - Call me an immature jabroni all you like but this is probably the most quote worthy comedy of all time. A toss-up between this or Wayne's World as to what is my favorite comedy. I still need to get to San Diego...

2. National Treasure (2004) - I am a treasure lover. While I am not a Nic Cage lover, he was tolerable and I loved the plot. I took my "Little Brother" through Big Brother/Big Sister to see this in the theater. He brought his sister and a friend. I always recall that random time I took three kids I barely knew to see National Treasure.

3. Dodgeball (2004) - The goofy ridiculous comedies were all the rage in this era and my maturity, or lack thereof, was a perfect fit. It also inspired many a dodgeball league that I would later participate in. "If you can dodge a wrench, you can dodge a ball."

4. Crash (2004) - What a downer after the top three, but this was well done and incredibly emotional. The kind of movie where it was so good, you're sad afterwards because you realized the world is a messed up place. It sticks with you.

5. Collateral (2004) - I really dug Tom Cruise as a bad guy and I am not an avid Tom Cruise supporter. In fact, I am not even a big fan of Jaime Foxx but the plot was very entertaining and performed well.

Movies from 2005 (C)

1. Wedding Crashers (2005) – Saw this one in theaters with my buddy Dusty when I lived in the Lou. Owen Wilson and Vince Vaughn both put up A+ performances. This was the breakout of Bradley Cooper as well. "The painting was a gift, Todd. I'm taking it with me."

2. 40 Year Old Virgin (2005) – Funny movie. Steven Carrell and Paul Rudd really make this for me. Great music/dance sequence at the film's conclusion. After this one, 2005 gets a bit sketchy.

3. The Lion, the Witch, and the Wardrobe (2005) – 2005 was a rough year for film. Crazy that this is my #3. I mean I love the *Chronicles of Narnia* as a book series, so I guess I have this on my list because of those books. Movie was solid. I really wanted to throat punch Edmund for most of the film however.

4. Kingdom of Heaven (2005) – Another just solid flick from 2005. I generally enjoy the topic of the Crusades. Orlando Bloom was ok. This movie went on longer than the Crusades...am I right?

5. Hitch (2005) – I'm shocked this is even on my list at all. Enjoyable film but nowhere near a favorite of any kind. I enjoyed the Fresh Prince and Eva Mendes. Kevin James is a barf encrusted jumbo jerk in this though. Fun Fact: I watched this for the first time at my cousin Cheryl's in Denver.

Movies from 2005 (L)

1. Wedding Crashers (2005) - I am a little depressed at how much of a sucker I am for crude humor. Owen Wilson and Vince Vaughn were gold and I don't care that neither have captured that same level since. Rachel McAdams is in it which doesn't hurt a thing either. Ferrell's cameo is spot on as well.

2. V for Vendetta (2005) - It was just so different than any other movie. Led me down a rabbit hole of studying the real Guy Fawkes. Portman was great. I saw this by myself while living in Florida before my wedding.

3. Star Wars III: Revenge of the Sith (2005) - Don't kid yourself, it isn't great. I attended a midnight showing of this one with my great friend Doug, so it has some sentimental value.

4. Brick (2005) - Gritty and Grimy indie movie that I bet many haven't seen. It is raw but Joseph Gordon-Levitt was great and there are some young actors in here who did a good job that ended up doing some good things down the road, including Claire from LOST. Hidden gem.

5. Kingdom of Heaven (2005) - I don't know how historically accurate this was but by now you know that I am a sucker for history. This just came to mind...What the heck happened to Orlando Bloom? Where did he go? Is he on a milk carton somewhere?

Movies from 2006 (C)

1. The Prestige (2006) – "Are you watching closely?" My favorite Christopher Nolan film, yea its way better than his Batman movies. Hugh Jackman and Christian Bale are wonderful in this. Who doesn't love a movie about magic that ends up being a Sci-Fi movie? Need I mention David Bowie is in this? Abracadabra.

2. Inside Man (2006) - This movie is awesome from the opening song all the way to the end. To be fair Clive Owen is really good but Denzel steals the show. I like the underlying story of the film where you wonder if Denzel is somewhat of a dirty cop. "This ain't no bank robbery."

3. Talladega Nights (2006) – Went to a Cardinals/Reds game in Cincinnati with some friends and to kill some time we saw Talladega Nights in the theater. I think I was the only one who truly enjoyed it as Will was getting a bit stale by then. Will and John C. Reilly were fantastic. Some great quotes and a very underrated cast. "If you don't chew Big Red gum then eff you."

4. The Departed (2006) – DiCaprio, Damon, Nicholson, Marky-Mark, Sheen and Baldwin...what a cast. Putting Dropkick Murphy's on the Soundtrack was a great tone setter for the film. Here's a question though...who is the actual main star of the film?

5. 300 (2006) - My buddy Nate and I saw this down in Fort Myer's, FL. This was visually breathtaking and I remember loving it at the time, but I haven't seen it since 2006. Yet it still finds its way to #5 for 2006.

Movies from 2006 (L)

1. The Prestige (2006) - Hot diggity dog. A masterpiece by Christopher Nolan before he blew up huge. Bale and Jackman were spot on. Love him or hate him, Bale brings it something fierce here. The ending sticks with you too. Pepper in the supporting cast that includes Caine and Bowie….Voila

2. Children of Men (2006) - A good raw and emotional story. A screenplay like none other. I always had a soft spot for Clive Owen as well and I can't quite explain it. I also remember reading that the climax was shot with an unstable hand cam and they used the one take. Might be bologna but I love that story regardless.

3. Half Nelson (2006) - A good year for raw and emotional lower budget dramas. Probably Ryan Gosling's best work that no one knows about. Sad tale that probably is accurate.

4. The Departed (2006) - You won't find a better cast (unless you add Affleck, right Casey?). The soundtrack was really special too. Also, it set the record for head shots within a three minute period of time.

5. Flags of our Fathers (2006) - For those three of you still reading this, you probably figured a history film would sneak in. I have really started digging WWII history more and more as I slowly become an old man, so this one plays even stronger today than it did in 2006.

Movies from 2007 (C)

1. Transformers (2007) - I was a huge Transformers cartoon fan in the 80's. I had been wanting this movie since the 90's and in 2007 my dream was coming true. Then I realized those movies you are often most excited for are terrible. I also wasn't a big Shia LaBeouf fan. I went in with very low expectations. I thought the film was fantastic and it flooded me with happy feelings. I will never forget it. I do however think I should have been involved in the script writing process. I had some better ideas.
2. 3:10 to Yuma (2007) - I'm a sucker for a good western and Russell Crowe is fantastic in this. Solid showing from Ben Foster as well. Christian Bale was ok.
3. Hot Fuzz (2007) – Not popular amongst my friends but I prefer Hot Fuzz to Shaun of the Dead (2004). I think it's funnier and just all around more entertaining. "Have you ever fired two guns whilst jumping through the air?"
4. National Treasure (2007) – Not a big Nic Cage fan...but I must give credit where credit is due. I feel like I've already said that a few times. I love history and treasure hunts...what can I say?
5. Superbad (2007) – The movie that gave us McLovin'. I don't know why but this feels like an updated License to Drive (1988). Bill Hader and Seth Rogen as the cops are my favorite characters. Fat Jonah Hill ain't no slouch either.

Movies from 2007 (L)

1. The Bourne Ultimatum (2007) - Not a news flash at this point but I adore the Bourne franchise. This was the rare occurrence where the third installment, to me at least, trumps them all. It ended fairly ambiguously but tightened things up in a great way where they could walk away if needed. The scene with Bourne in Vohsen's office is money.

2. Into the Wild (2007) - I watched this alone late one night while Allison traveled for work. I just sat there at the end dumbfounded, moved, and deep in thought. I think sometimes that is the feeling of a good film. 10 years later, I can vividly recall where I was and how I felt when it was over. Still can't believe it was based on a true story.

3. 3:10 to Yuma (2007) - The best modern western in my opinion. This had it all. Noble hero, likable villain and justice for some scoundrels. Not everyone gets out alive in the wild wild west and I loved the way they ended it.

4. No Country for Old Men (2007) - I so vividly remember peeing my pants (ok, maybe not quite, but close!) every time Javier Bardem appeared on screen. The movie was so different that I was happy to overlook some of the nontraditional qualities of the film. A great cast as well including Sir Tommy Lee Jones....pretty sure he is knighted.

5. Gone Baby Gone (2007) - Raw thriller that sadly brings up a lot of social and economic issues of our time. Of course Ben Affleck's involvement is a major benefit as he is a far superior talent to Ray Liotta. Long story......Maybe book 2.

Movies from 2008 (C)

1. Role Models (2008) – One of the funnier movies as of late. Paul Rudd teams with Stifler to bring us a LARP (Live Action Role Play)/KISS centric comedy? Yea that's right and it's phenomenal.

2. Iron Man (2008) - The original Iron Man was great. Felt like the return of Robert Downey Jr. He's such a great wise cracking protagonist. This also paved the way for the Marvel Universe. Had Iron Man not been such a hit we never would have had 723 superheroes movies. Also the sequels are garbage.

3. Step Brothers (2008) – Will Ferrell and John C. Reilly as you guessed it...step brothers. These two were great together in Talladega Nights (2006) and this was no different. This is probably the tail end of Will being funny though. "Chewbacca masks! It's ok that mine's not movie quality."

4. The Dark Knight (2008) – It's already been stated that I prefer Batman 89 and Nicholson will always be my Joker. But man Heath Ledger was phenomenal in his own right in the role. Ledger definitively carries the film and immediately makes it 100 times more interesting than Batman Begins (2005). It's a shame the role impacted Ledger the way it did but no one can ever question his dedication to the craft.

5. The Curious Case of Benjamin Button (2008) - This is a great story. They took a great concept and delivered. But it's so depressing when you realize Brad and Cate's relationship days are numbered. Also to be noted, my wife called this movie "emotionally mute" after I nearly cried.

Movies from 2008 (L)

1. The Wrestler (2008) - If there was ever a movie made for Luke Worrell, this might be it. I can't believe how great Mickey Rourke was in this movie. The Springsteen main score was pure emotion and I can barely get through the song. Dynamic stuff here with Ring of Honor and wrestling terminology sprinkled in...love it.

2. The Dark Knight (2008) - I feel like this brought the super hero movie back for me. They had become a dime a dozen honestly, but this was different and electric. Yes, Christian Bale's Batman voice is annoying but I can look past it. Plus there's Heath Ledger's Joker...

3. In Bruges (2008) - I am shocked I liked this movie to be honest. One of my pet peeves is the over usage of cursing and this movie had roughly 3,107 F bombs. I was going to be traveling to Bruges a few months before seeing this so I was captivated. The city itself is gorgeous and my visit there only cemented this movie in my mind.

4. The Hurt Locker (2008) - A raw movie without a big budget but it packed a punch. Jeremy Renner burst on the scene here and it was good stuff. Kate Austin from LOST shows up so I marked out for that pretty hard.

5. Step Brothers (2008) - I am a sucker for Will Ferrell. This was his normal ridiculousness but John C Reilly was an ingredient I didn't know I needed. One of the first things I think about is their plea for space so they can do "activities."

Movies from 2009 (C)

1. The Hangover (2009) – My wife and I saw this in the theater on a whim. I basically had no expectations going in. Great flick with some lasting quotes. Zach Galifianakis stole the show but then we had to put up with future Galifianakis movies. I'm sure this movie inspired a lot of dumb guy Vegas trips. "Tigers love pepper, they hate cinnamon."

2. Sherlock Holmes (2009) – Caught this one at the dollar theater, before my town tore the theater down to put up luxury student apartments...idiots. I don't know why I didn't have interest in this movie at first, I love the Sherlock character. I was late to the party but so glad I caught it in a theater. Robert Downey Jr. really shined. Wrestler Alert: Kurrgan

3. Angels and Demons (2009) – The book is so much better, but the film is pretty good as well. I was shocked I liked the Ewan McGregor role so much. Has nothing to do with the movie but I remember reading the entire book during a college spring baseball trip.

4. Watchmen (2009) – I had not read the graphic novel before watching the film. This was basically the first I had heard of the Watchmen. Thought it was great however I saw this with my dad (as an adult) and the sex scene set to "Hallelujah" was a little awkward. Great soundtrack.

5. I Love You Man (2009) – Another one I saw in the theater with the wifey. She's a big Paul Rudd fan (as am I) being from KC. Another film I wasn't expecting much from but it was pretty darn good. Big Rashida Jones fan as well. "What's up Joben?"

Movies from 2009 (L)

1. 500 Days of Summer (2009) - I love this movie. I love it so much that I don't know how to articulate that in just a few short sentences. I will say two things. One, I think Joseph Gordon-Levitt is grossly underrated. Two, Shirley from "Community" with a cameo. Don't miss it.

2. The Hangover (2009) - This one was so funny that I didn't even bother watching the subsequent films. That sounds counterintuitive but no way could they compare. Ten years later and I think this is still top notch dumb and raunchy gold.

3. Sherlock Holmes (2009) - Just a good old fashioned fun movie. I watched this on Christmas day with my dad. Entirely enjoyable and I liked the revamp. Darn that Robert Downey Jr. and his charisma.

4. Avatar (2009) - Unlike anything ever done before or since. I can see why it had an enormous budget. Side rant...How is Disney's Animal Kingdom just now making rides based on this film? I also feel it appropriate to now let everyone know that I think James Cameron is a chump. None the less, it is on the list.

5. Zombieland (2009) - Bill Murray's cameo alone has this list worthy. Woody Harrelson is just plain good and Jesse Eisenberg and Emma Stone are both super talented as well. It was cool to see a "zombie" movie be a comedy and not a laughable "B movie" horror show.

Movies from 2010 (C)

1. Hot Tub Time Machine (2010) – Went to see this in the theater with basically no expectations. This is probably my top comedy in the last 10 years. Rob Cordry is hilarious and John Cusack doesn't ruin it. If you know me, I love all things 80's, so this movie is right up my alley. I like to pretend the sequel doesn't exist. "Great white buffalo."

2. Inception (2010) – This is one of those movies that you have to pay full attention to if you expect to understand. If you check your phone for like one second...you're lost. This movie is such a great concept and I like most of the cast. The Leo and Marion Cotillard storyline bums me out though. Saw this in theaters the night before I left for Germany...won't forget that.

3. Shutter Island (2010) – Good year for Leo. Read the book first and really enjoyed it. Saw the film and enjoyed it just as much as the book. A lot of similarities to his Inception character. You never know what's real or not.

4. True Grit (2010) – At first a John Wayne remake seemed sacrilegious but then I saw the film and loved it. Only "The Dude" could pull off the "The Duke". Well done film. Also to be noted, the girl in the new one wasn't super annoying like in the original.

5. The Expendables (2010) – Guilty pleasure of mine. Total meatball movie but it's actually pretty damn entertaining. I actually enjoy the entire Expendables franchise. Stallone keeps delivering. Keep them coming Sly, but next time include Kurt Russell and Hulk Hogan...Brother!

Movies from 2010 (L)

1. Inception (2010) - One of the most mind numbing movies ever made. Cast was sensational, soundtrack impactful and that screenplay was exquisite. Ok, I am not sure exquisite is an appropriate adjective but I am going to roll with it. I saw this twice in the theater. A rarity in modern times.

2. The Town (2010) - Even if you took out the super talented Ben Affleck, this movie was great. Jeremy Renner stole the show but the remaining cast delivered from start to finish. I don't love the end but I can live with it based on how great the rest of the movie was. I will say that it doesn't help Boston in my eyes, but that might also be mostly because of the Patriots and Red Sox.

3. Shutter Island (2010) - I had grave concerns that they would do a disservice to the book. One of the few times, I was pleasantly surprised when seeing a movie after a great book. I am not a big Leo guy but apparently he killed it in 2010. I know this is a movie list book but the book itself, holy moly. I almost couldn't read it when the sun was down.

4. Winter's Bone (2010) - An indie darling of 2010 and the coming out party of Jennifer Lawrence. Not to be overlooked is how good John Hawkes was in this movie. He killed it. I really dig these gritty and raw indie movies and this was one of the best in recent memory.

5. Date Night (2010) - I feel like this movie got lost in the shuffle of a really cinematically strong 2010. I think it also might be because the movie Date Night was just that for me. I remember Allison and I having a really great "Date Night" based around this movie. Oh the irony...

Movies from 2011 (C)

1. Horrible Bosses (2011) – Hilarious movie. I'm hot and cold on Jason Sudeikis but I love Jason Bateman. Charlie Day has his moments as well, but as a collective unit they were fantastic. I feel like the Kevin Spacey character in this movie is the real life Kevin Spacey. Seems like he could be a jerk face in real life. Maybe Jennifer Anniston's finest on screen moment was in this film.

2. Bridesmaids (2011) – Good year for comedy. Kristen Wiig is great and she dominates this movie. Good coming out film for Melissa McCarthy as well. I always, ALWAYS enjoy the mom from the Goldbergs. Also to be noted I like Wilson Phillips.

3. The Muppets (2011) – Who doesn't love the Muppets? Seriously tell me because I will fight them. Thank the heavens for Jason Segel and his love for the Muppets, he single handedly got this movie made. The music is A+ and in the true Muppets spirit they had some great cameos. My only critique is that Pepe the King Prawn only had one scene. I also remember seeing this with my 9-month pregnant wife at the time.

4. Moneyball (2011) – Not good enough for my baseball movie list but still a good movie. I typically love Brad Pitt movies…and then when you factor in baseball…I'm locked in. This film was great exposure for Chris Pratt who is a Scott Hatteberg doppelganger. Great film about the unique approach the front office took to building a team but the film forgets to mention the A's had three phenomenal starting pitchers at the time.

5. Your Highness (2011) – Guilty pleasure. Overall pretty silly movie. You James Franco and Danny McBride fans will enjoy it. It's a basically a funnier, cruder Knights Tale (2001) of sorts. I saw this in theaters with my buddy Noah and he has the kind of laugh that is super infectious. So every time I watch this at home (by

myself) I still hear Noah laughing in my head. The minotaur scene is something to behold.

Movies from 2011 (L)
1. Bridesmaids (2011) - This is kind of like the female Anchorman (2004) for me. Hilarity at every turn and one quotable line after another. We are huge Wiig fans and love us some Ellie Kemper as well (Yay Kimmy Schmidt!)
2. The Help (2011) - A great year for female casts apparently. This was an incredibly powerful movie. The cast was top notch. As much I love Chastain and enjoy Emma Stone, Bryce Dallas Howard was not a nice lady. She was such a good heel character that it made the film 5 times more impactful.
3. Midnight in Paris (2011) - This honestly might be the only Woody Allen film I have ever watched. Heaven help me I love Paris, Owen Wilson and even the beautiful Rachel McAdams. The movie makes Paris pop so it has huge sentimental value to me.
4. Moneyball (2011) - I vividly remember buying the book Moneyball at "The Coop", the Harvard bookstore while traveling in Boston. Never in a million years would I have imagined that it would be made into a movie, starring Brad Pitt none-the-less. It was like an odd dream watching this movie come to life. Still though, they couldn't have mentioned that they had three stud pitchers? Zito, Hudson and Mulder were ghosts in the movie and rarely mentioned in the book either.
5. Ides of March (2011) - I am surprised this wasn't a bigger hit with Clooney and Gosling at the helm. Sleazy political drama that is probably more accurate than we would like to believe. I watched this in Charleston, SC. Really dug it.

Movies from 2012 (C)

1. Avengers (2012) - Great concept...all the superheroes teaming up together for one movie? Well played. Tip of the cap. Saw this in theaters and I'll never forget laughing out loud when Hulk starts whipping Loki around like a rag doll.
2. Skyfall (2012) – My favorite Daniel Craig Bond movie. Felt like a good mix of modern Bond mixed with some good call backs to the Bond of old. Adele's "Skyfall" has to be up there for best Bond song as well. I enjoyed Casino Royale (2006) but Quantum of Solace (2008) and Spectre (2015) were dog turds.
3. 21 Jump Street (2012) – I watched the original show every day before swim lessons for what seemed like an entire summer. I tried to temper my excitement and I was a little worried when Channing Tatum was cast. Turned out to be a funny movie. And Jonah Hill was skinny in this...WTH?
4. The Hobbit (2012) – Went to see this on my birthday in 2012, I know that because my boss at the time called me a nerd for doing so. Anyhow, I loved the book and I loved the Lord of the Rings series...was a no brainer. Unfortunately the other two Hobbit movies were not good. Should have just been one movie.
5. Prometheus (2012) – I know Alien/Aliens fans love to hate this movie...but I actually really enjoyed it. It really could stand alone as its own movie, being a sort of prequel to the Alien franchise put a lot of added pressure on the film. It's better than Alien: Covenant (2017).

Movies from 2012 (L)

1. Zero Dark Thirty (2012) - This has continually popped up on my lists. I love the trailer. I love the story. I love the cast. I love the psychology of it all.
2. Lincoln (2012) - I live in Springfield. I am pretty sure legally I have to have this on my list. One of the world's best actors playing the icon that is Abe Lincoln, directed by Spielberg. I mean come on...
3. Skyfall (2012) - I think this was the best Bond movie of the new era. Dame Judy Dench was spot on and Javier Bardem is a classic Bond bad guy. It had everything a Bond film should have. A personal memory of mine is watching this over Christmas with family from Europe. Bond is truly global.
4. End of Watch (2012) - What a nut punch this movie was. I watched this alone in Denver after taking my AFM exam. I was crumbled over in emotion when the credits rolled. I really enjoyed the way it was shot. I remember sadly walking next door to a Qdoba after the movie was over to drown my emotions with queso.
5. Argo (2012) - The one and only Ben Affleck ladies and gentlemen. Great movie even if Canada is ticked about not getting enough love. I really didn't know much about the historical context of the film so it was like being entertained but going to school all in one. Ray Liotta can't direct a commercial, let alone an Oscar worthy movie.

*This is where Luke started having kids and is way behind on his movies. His selections for 2013-2017 will come in the next edition of the book.

Movies from 2013 (C)
1. Now You See Me (2013) – 2013 was kind of a down year for me. Now You See Me was my top movie of the year. Very enjoyable. It was something different. My wife loves Woody Harrelson. But I'd never list it as a favorite of any kind anywhere other than this list.
2. This is the End (2013) – Pretty funny flick but super dark. This movie is pretty uncomfortable at times. The references to the Pineapple Express sequel are fantastic. Danny McBride is great as well.
3. We're the Millers (2013) – Well it has Jennifer Anniston...and it's funny. That's all I have on this one.
4. Captain Phillips (2013) – Pretty intense flick starring the one and only Tom Hanks. The actor who played the main pirate was really good! Knowing this was a true story helped but finding out the Captain wasn't respected by the crew really hurt it.
5. Thor 2: Dark World (2013) – I liked this one better than the original and I'm so excited to see Ragnarok. I love the atmosphere of Asgard. Loki is a great frienemy.

Movies from 2014 (C)

1. American Sniper (2014) - It's a good mix of story and intense action. Bradley Cooper should have received an Oscar. I've never left the theater in such a sobering mood. There was absolute silence as everyone sauntered out of the theater.

2. Guardians of the Galaxy (2014) – Up there for my favorite Marvel movie. I like the sequel a tad more but the first one is just as awesome. I love the feel of these movies. They look different and sound different than most superhero movies. This flick really helped save the superhero genre in my opinion. Chris Pratt was awesome and this is definitely Vin Diesel's best performance...I mean he shows the most range in this flick than any other in his career. Also Drax was comic gold (Dave Bautista – Wrestler).

3. Edge of Tomorrow (2014) – Ugh...I can't quit you Tom Cruise. Just to be clear I don't want to like Tom Cruise but I can't stop being entertained by his films. I loved this storyline. It's basically a futuristic war version of Groundhog Day (1993). Emily Blunt was glorious.

4. The Equalizer (2014) – What could be better than seeing a mild mannered Denzel Washington beat up a bunch of jerks? That's a rhetorical question. This movie is very simple...and awesome!

5. Gone Girl (2014) – This movie terrifies me. Crazy girlfriends are scarier than Pennywise the clown. Normally I hate Affleck but even I feel for him in this movie. Rosamund Pike deserved an Oscar for this performance.

Movies from 2015 (C)

1. Jurassic World (2015) – Finally a good Jurassic Park sequel. Great idea with the execution of the Jurassic World theme park. Thought it was really cool to see tourists in the park and to see the attractions. The Mosasaurus ruled. How cheesy was the raptor nodding at Chris Pratt at the end though? Great LEGO tie in game that my son "got" me for Father's Day as well.

2. Furious 7 (2015) – Probably my favorite of the franchise. I've never seen a franchise that keeps getting better with age (excluding the eighth addition). Great move in adding Kurt Russell to the cast. Wrestler alert...The Rock

3. Bridge of Spies (2015) - A more recent Spielberg flick that I really enjoyed. Nice mix of drama and humor, and I felt like this was Tom's best performance in quite some time.

4. Hateful Eight (2015) – Took my two brother-in-laws to see this in the theater. Neither of them were big Tarantino fans, so I don't think they loved the overly gratuitous blood. Had a real The Thing (1982) vibe. Spoiler alert: Killed me to see Kurt go down in this one.

5. Mad Max: Fury Road (2015) – Saw this in theaters with my buddy Jason. Great movie experience. One of those films where the theater enhances the experience. Tom Hardy did nothing for me. Charlize Theron was fantastic though.

Movies from 2016 (C)

1. Deadpool (2016) – Just a well done movie. It was unlike any other superhero movie out there. Ryan Reynolds is the perfect Deadpool. They did a great job of sticking with the "R" rating and really going for it. The opening credits really set the tone. "Listen, we both know that cancer is a shit-show. Like a Yakov Smirnoff opening for the Spin Doctors at the Iowa State Fair shit-show."

2. Hacksaw Ridge (2016) – This was a really moving story and well told. The true story factor makes it even better. Andrew Garfield was fantastic. Good to see Vince Vaughn doing something worthwhile again.

3. La La Land (2016) – Took my wife to see this in theaters. She had been wanting to see it so badly. Coming away I think I liked it better. Gosling and Stone clearly have great onscreen chemistry. Cool story with some good tunes. They were robbed of the Oscar...literally.

4. Rogue One (2016) – Really enjoyed Rogue One. Felt like a Star Wars "war" movie. This movie had real stakes. K-2SO stole the show. Definitely not a kids' movie.

5. 13 Hours (2016) – Politics aside this movie was incredible. I was on the edge of my seat the whole time. Also weird seeing Jim Halpert as a "professional soldier", but he was totally believable. Another Office tidbit to be noted: Pam's ex-boyfriend, Roy, is also in the movie.

Movies from 2017 (C)

1. **Guardians of the Galaxy 2 (2017)** - Another instance where I liked it better than the original. I love the emotion of this movie! Maybe it's because I am a father myself, but I really dug the father/son story. It really hit me in the feels. Another killer soundtrack. It was also great to see that old school Dairy Queen at the beginning.

2. **Baby Driver (2017)** – Just watched this a few weeks ago. 1) Baby stole my look. I've been rocking the hooded jacket and ear buds for years. 2) I wasn't sure what I was really expecting...but the ending was absolutely nuts. Some good jams featured as well.

3. **The Big Sick (2017)** – Threw this on the DVD queue for my wife. We watched it recently and I'll be damned, it was a good movie. Kumail Nanjiani is freakin' hilarious for starters then you factor in a very non-conventional love story. It was great to see Ray Romano doing something other than a wooly mammoth voice as well.

4. **Baywatch (2017)** – Baywatch was so dumb...but I love that they all went for it. I'll never say a bad word about the Rock (Dwayne Johnson) and not because he would destroy me but because I think he is entertaining as hell. Zac Efron was also fantastic in this flick. Yes there were some cringe worthy moments in this film, but on the whole, I thought it was a fun summer flick.

5. **Thor: Ragnarok (2017)** - Saw this in theaters. I'm going to leave it at #5 edging out Blade Runner 2049 and Wonder Woman but really this could have been #2 on the list. Felt like they borrowed a bit from the Guardians movies (which was smart) in the film's tone and 80's feel. Heard that Big Trouble in Little China was a major influence as well, which warms my heart. Korg may be the best character of the movie.